Coursework GCSE Mathematics

George Bujewicz
Barry Greenwood
Glenys Ward
Ted Ward

Causeway Press

Teachers' Introduction

This book is a practical guide for pupils doing coursework assignments. It is designed to introduce pupils to the skills and techniques required for the coursework component of GCSE Mathematics. The book covers the main features of the guidelines and recommendations for coursework given by the various GCSE examining consortia. It is presented in such a way that the students will have an insight into what is expected of them and how they will be assessed for GCSE.

The guidance given in this book is applicable to extended pieces of work of a practical and investigative kind as proposed in the National Curriculum. The text is interspersed with a large number of short exercises which aim to encourage students to develop and practise the skills used in practical assignments. In addition to the section devoted to examples of assignment tasks, there is a wide range of ideas scattered throughout the book which can be developed into coursework projects.

The GCSE National Criteria for Mathematics stresses the importance of students developing their mathematical abilities by solving problems and conducting individual and cooperative enquiry and experiment. The aim of this book is to guide the student in planning, investigating and presenting coursework. It provides a framework for study, giving support and guidance to the less able and a stimulus for the more able. It is hoped that the book can be used in a variety of ways: read through and discussed rather like a traditional textbook; issued to pupils to work through at their own pace; or used selectively by pupils whenever they need help with a particular aspect of coursework.

Causeway Press Ltd
PO Box 13, Ormskirk, Lancashire L39 5HP

© George Bujewicz, Barry Greenwood,
  Glenys Ward, Ted Ward. 1989

First published 1989

British Library Cataloguing in Publication Data

Coursework in GCSE mathematics.
  1. Mathematics. – For schools
  I. Bujewicz, George
  510

  ISBN 0-946183-49-X

Designed and produced by The Art Factory
Illustrations and cartoons by Howard Prescott

Typesetting by Chapterhouse, Formby, L37 3PX

Printed and bound by The Alden Press, Oxford.

Contents

Teachers' Introduction

Section A: What is courework, why do it?   4

Section B: Starting your assignment
    Part 1. Finding an idea   10
    Part 2. Choosing an idea   23
    Part 3. Getting going   24

Section C: Collection of data
    Part 1. What data do I need?   34
    Part 2. How to collect data   39

Section D: Representation of data   58

Section E: Analysis and Explanation   86

Section F: Putting it all together
    Part 1. Assignment planner   112
    Part 2. Carrying out the task   115
    Part 3. Writing up your task   118

Section G: Assignment tasks.   120

Acknowledgements

The authors and publishers would like to thank the following for permission to reproduce copyright material, photographs and artwork.

Wolverhampton council (Photo p.5)
Liverpool Daily Post & Echo (Photo p.6, p.17)
Drive Publications Ltd (Photo p.7 reproduced from 'Illustrated Guide to Britain')
Yorkshire TV. (Photo p.11)
Associated Press Ltd (Photo p.9)
M. Haralambos (Photo p.12)
Leisurewire UK Ltd (Photo p.12, p.22, Illustrations of their construction kit Plawco.)
M. McLachlan (p.19 from the 'What if?' pack)
Tees Sport Ltd (Photo p.21)
H. Prescott (Photo p.22)
Daily Telegraph plc (Extract p.92)
Tarquin publications (Photo p.14)
Howard Davies, Sandpiper Rd., Wigan (Photo p.17)

Every effort has been made to locate the copyright owners of material included. Any omissions brought to the publisher's attention are regretted and will be credited in subsequent printings.

> In its broadest sense, mathematics coursework is all the work you do throughout your course in mathematics.

Coursework is:

- Investigating: asking your own questions.
- Problem solving: looking at problems inside and outside the classroom.
- Practical work: experiments and model making.
- The opportunity to do extended pieces of work.

This book is about '**coursework tasks**'.

> But what is a coursework task?

Is it:

- A task you have done by yourself in class?
- Work you have completed as a member of a group?
- An assignment set by the teacher or the examination board?
- An investigation/experiment you have carried out away from the classroom?
- A project you may have been set?
- A piece of work to be done by yourself at home?

It can be any of these – it is work done during your GCSE course which counts towards your final mark.

WHAT IS COURSEWORK, WHY DO IT?

But why should I bother doing them?

Let's look at some of the advantages which coursework can offer.

Coursework can make mathematics real.

Mathematics becomes real when you apply what you learn in school to a variety of situations.

Example Unemployment in the city. You could have explored this real problem in the following way.

In a study of unemployment in the city you might be concerned with collecting statistics about youth and adult unemployment in the inner city, comparing them with similar statistics for the suburbs. You could also produce statistics comparing the length of unemployment for different age and/or gender groups.

Young unemployed in Wolverhampton

Often problems in the real world are not as simple to solve as those given in textbooks.

Exercise 1
Make a list of the mathematical ideas you could explore in this real situation. Constructing the most direct route for a proposed new stretch of motorway.

Some people are really good at working through written exercises and can explain exactly what they are doing. Other people are not. It's not fair to expect everybody to be able to show how much they know or understand by just working through written examples.

Coursework can let you show off.

GCSE
COURSEWORK
"ALL MY
OWN WORK
AND IDEAS"

Example Curves. Suppose you were set an assignment to explore curved shapes in everyday life. Your work could be illustrated by using photographs of shapes such as radio telescopes and cooling towers. You could make scale drawings of orbits and use spirographs to create imaginative patterns. You can show everybody concerned how much you know about the curved shapes that occur in everyday life, and how much work you have done.

Radio-Telescope – Jodrell Bank

Exercise 2

Suppose you were investigating the different ways of investing money. Describe briefly the mathematics you would use and how you could show people how knowledgeable you are.

Coursework makes mathematics more interesting.

Coursework allows you to follow an interest and develop it.

■WHAT IS COURSEWORK, WHY DO IT?

Example The construction industry. Suppose you were interested in the construction industry. How might this interest be developed for coursework in mathematics?

You could decide to explore the construction of a medieval castle complete with moat and bailey. This could involve lots of measurement and scale drawing.

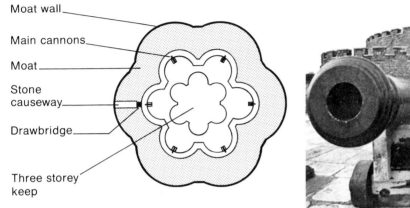

Moat wall

Main cannons

Moat

Stone causeway

Drawbridge

Three storey keep

Deal Castle – Tudor rose design

Exercise 3

Make a list of the mathematics topics you would need to know to set up a mini-business at school.

Coursework gives you the freedom to find out what you want to know.

Some parts of the GCSE course may interest you more than others and you may want to find out more about a particular topic in mathematics.

Coursework gives you the freedom to study a topic in greater depth.

Example Working in a bank. Suppose you want to work in a bank when you leave school and at present you are learning about percentages, interest and currency exchange. You could do yourself a favour by investigating how these calculations are used in a bank.

Exercise 4

Choose a topic from your mathematics syllabus that particularly interests you. Briefly discuss how it could help you in future employment.

In all your subjects you will have to use certain skills, such as written communication, discussion, research techniques, speaking clearly, etc. You can use coursework in mathematics to develop these skills

I LIKE WRITING

I HATE DRAWING!

I'M HOPELESS IN A DEBATE – I GET REALLY ANGRY AND STOP LISTENING TO PEOPLE

'My Mum says that the posters on my bedroom wall show real artistic flair!'

I ♥ TALKING TO PEOPLE

my spelling is ~~tenible~~ terrible

I'M A WIZARD WITH A CAMERA

Coursework helps you to develop important skills.

Example Talking about mathematics. In GCSE English you may be assessed on your ability to give a short speech. You can practise this by giving a talk about your coursework task to your group. Illustrate it with pictures, photographs and charts to make it more interesting.

Exercise 5
Think about your own communication skills. What can you do best?

Coursework encourages you to make links between mathematics and other subjects.

Example Projects in other subjects. By doing a project on machines you could incorporate ideas from Control Technology, CDT, Humanities and Science.

Exercise 6
Choose one of your GCSE subjects and discuss briefly how mathematics could help you develop a project in that subject.

Coursework lets you job share.

Example Conducting a survey. Sometimes collecting information can be time consuming. If, when conducting a statistical survey using a questionnaire you tackle this as a group, you will finish it more quickly and you might even have some fun!

WHAT IS COURSEWORK, WHY DO IT?

Coursework helps you to put the course together.

When you are studying different parts of the GCSE mathematics syllabus the whole course is broken down into a series of separate topics. Coursework can help to fit the topics together.

Example Space travel. You may have been studying angles, properties of 2D and 3D shapes, enlargement and similarity, trigonometry – all separate topics.
An assignment exploring space travel could bring all these topics together.

Space shuttle – Discovery 1988

So you see coursework tasks can take a variety of forms. They can be done throughout the 4th and 5th year and the time taken to do them will vary according to the task . . . a lesson, a lesson and homework, a week, even longer.

What is the value of coursework?

It can:
- Make mathematics come to life.
- Help you to solve problems in the outside world.
- Give you the opportunity to apply mathematics to your own interests and hobbies.
- Provide links between mathematics and your other subjects, and between school and work.
- Give you the opportunity to think for yourself.
- Give you the chance to show what you are good at.
- Help you to develop skill in communication.
- Encourage argument, originality, and creativity.

Now you have an idea about what coursework is you should try it for yourselves. The rest of this book will show you how it should be done.

SECTION B

Part 1 Finding an idea

As you work through the exercises in this section you can build up a collection or **resource bank** of ideas that you can draw upon for your coursework.

STARTING YOUR ASSIGNMENT

Let's look more closely for ideas.

Measuring the Earth's circumference – Eratosthenes' method

At school

1 Course content so far

You have studied mathematics since primary school. There are many aspects of your mathematical education which could be developed into a piece of coursework. You could select a puzzle, problem or topic that you have found interesting.

Example 1 Measurement. The study of units of measurement from the past to the present.

Example 2 Volume. Look at familiar objects around you; a jam jar, an apple, an orange, a gold fish bowl, a fish tank, a bath. Investigating methods of finding their volume would make an interesting coursework task.

> **Exercise 1**
> Make a list of at least 5 things you have studied in Mathematics and found interesting, e.g. Similarity.
> Now choose 3 that you found the most interesting and briefly explain how each of them could be developed further.
> You may find it easier to work with a friend or in a group.

2 Other courses you may be following

You may be surprised to find how much mathematics there is in some of your other subjects. Now you can look at them in a different way – for mathematical coursework ideas.
For example, think about tessellation, symmetry and pattern in Art; ratio, plans and scale models in Craft, Design and Technology; statistics in Business Studies, Sociology and Economics; measurement in Home Economics.

Example From C. D. T. Making a screwdriver involves conversion of fractions to decimals, multiplication and division, use of conversion tables, ratio, π, and using formulae.

> ### Exercise 2
> Choose 3 of your option courses. Compile a list of as many mathematical ideas as you can find in each one.

At home

1 Interests and hobbies

These can be a good source of ideas. You may be interested in sport, stamp collecting, model making, embroidery, TV. Coursework allows you to pursue your interest in school time!

Using a computer at home

Example 1 Watching television. How can you turn this into a piece of coursework?

- You could find out how much time is given each week to your favourite type of programme – sport, soaps, films, – on your favourite channel or all channels.
- Do all channels give equal time to your favourite programmes?
- How does this compare with the time given to programmes you dislike?
- You might like to find out about other people's favourite programmes

Mathematical areas to explore through television could be time, percentage and statistics.

Example 2 Model making. To build a model aircraft, obtain a picture or plan of a plane (from a magazine or your holiday aircraft). The coursework would then involve ratio, proportion, scale drawing, and if you wish the plane to fly, the mechanics of flight.

Exercise 3

Work in a group and make a list of everybody's interests and hobbies. List the mathematical ideas connected with these interests and hobbies. Suggest briefly how some of these could be developed into a piece of coursework.

2 Newspapers and magazines

These often carry headlines or articles which spark off ideas. Here are a few suggestions to explore through newspapers and magazines.

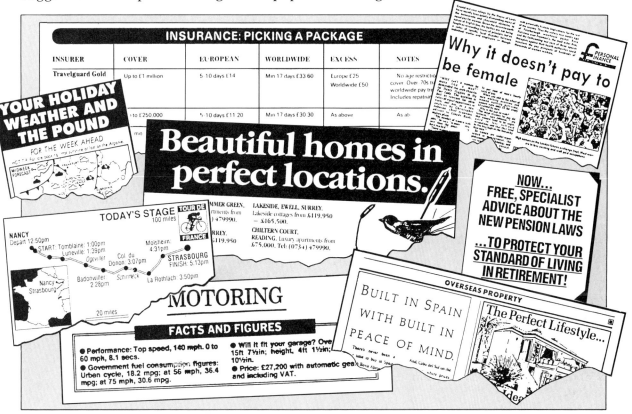

Example 1 Advertisements. You could look through advertisements for house sales in your local paper and compare prices with the size of the house and the areas in which they are located.

Example 2 Holidays. You might like to investigate holidays, comparing the cost of similar holidays offered by different travel companies.

Exercise 4

Look through a newspaper and make a list of at least 5 topics which you could use for coursework tasks. Explain briefly how they could be developed.

SECTION B

Example 3 Newspaper contents. Use the newspaper or magazine itself as the basis for your coursework.

You could:

- Choose a topic that interests you, say, sport, fashion, etc. Examine how the amount of coverage it receives compares with other topics. You could do this for a week or longer.
- Compare the 'look' of two very different newspapers, e.g. *The Sun* and *The Guardian*. Look at articles, photographs, headlines, size of print and so on. Present your results mathematically, e.g. size of photographs, number of words per page, number of columns etc.
- Examine tables, statistics and graphs which appear over a week. Consider how they are constructed, how they should be interpreted, what information do they give, do they mislead the reader?

Outside

The world is full of geometrical curves, surfaces, shapes and designs.

1 Nature

Look at:

    – ripples on a pond
    – scales on a fish
    – symmetry in a butterfly
    – design in snowflakes.

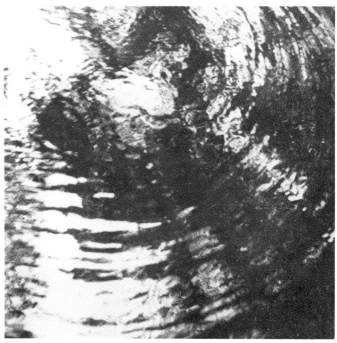

Ripples on a pond

Through nature you could explore such mathematical topics as symmetry, proportion, perspective, ratio, pattern, spirals and curves.

Exercise 5
Look up information on 'mathematics in nature' and write down briefly some ideas which you could investigate for possible coursework tasks.

2 Man-made objects

Look at:

- the triangles on pylons
- the construction of the pyramids
- the curves used for bridge construction
- the shape of cooling towers.

Electricity pylon

Exercise 6

Choose any three man-made objects. Write briefly how each might be developed into a coursework task.

> There are many other areas where you could get ideas for coursework tasks. Industry, famous mathematicians, other cultures, ancient times. I'm sure you can think of others now!

Exercise 7

Make a list of as many areas as you can which might provide ideas for coursework tasks.

More ideas for ideas

So far you have **looked at** different subjects – Art, C. D. T., Home Economics etc., as a source for coursework ideas. You have **looked at** home, school and outside.

Now try a different starting point. Instead of asking 'Where shall I **look**?' ask 'What shall I **do?**' This question can provide lots of ideas for coursework.

Why not consider:

- discovering patterns
- making models
- carrying out a survey
- organising an event
- carrying out an experiment?

You might like discovering patterns

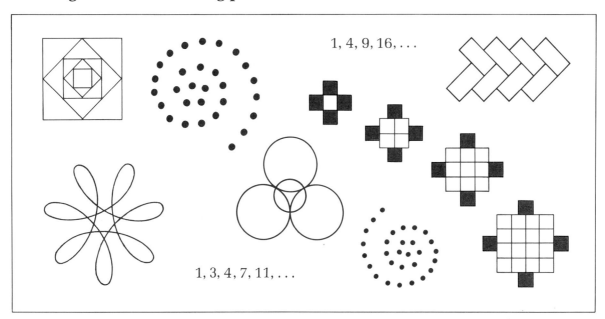

Number patterns

If a set of numbers can be arranged in a regular sequence they form a number pattern, e.g. 2, 4, 6, 8, . . .

Example. Suppose you were investigating the pattern formed if you add two consecutive triangular numbers in sequence. This task can be illustrated with diagrams involving geometric patterns and the areas of squares.

Spiral patterns

Example. You may be interested in counting the spirals on a pine cone, a pineapple or the centre part of a sunflower. You could then look for links with Fibonacci numbers (you can discover more about Fibonacci numbers from your textbook).

Wallpaper design

Example. Why not obtain several samples of wallpaper and look for examples of symmetry, tessellations and transformations in their design?

Curves (loci)

Example. You might want to investigate the parabola, which is the curve of the quadratic function. You could make a cone from modelling clay. Discover how to slice the cone to reveal a surface which is the shape of a parabola. Does the parabola occur naturally? This could be extended to its 3-dimensional applications for mirrors, TV aerials and modern architecture.

Geometric patterns

Example. Why not look at old buildings in your nearest town and compare them with modern structures? You could take photographs and draw diagrams of the geometric patterns used in the architecture. Look closely at floors and ceilings as they provide good examples of the use of geometric shapes.

Metropolitan Cathedral (Liverpool)

Anglican Cathedral (Liverpool)

Exercise 8

Take each of these headings: number pattern, spiral patterns, wallpaper design, curves and geometric patterns. For each, list ideas that could be developed into a piece of coursework. (Look at your textbooks and library books for suggestions.)

You might like making models

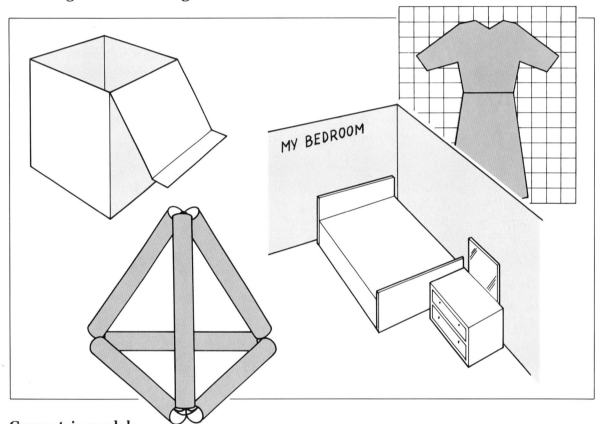

Geometric models

Example. You may like to study the 'Five Platonic Solids' (look them up in your mathematics library books). Why not imagine you have landed on the planet 'Hedron' and build models of the types of structures you could expect to find there?

Models from nets

Example. If you consider the net of a cube, how many different shaped nets can you draw? You may like to try to construct a cube from a rectangular piece of paper by cutting it into two identical pieces. Need the cut be straight or can it be curved?

Scale models

Example. You could make a dress for a doll by copying a full size dress. This would involve ratio, proportion, scale drawing and of course needlework.

Origami

Example. Why not make some paper models? Many textbooks and library books show how to make paper models. These provide lots of geometric and trigonometric ideas for investigations.

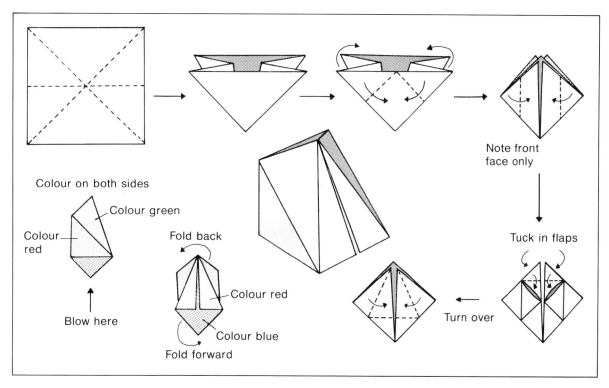

Exercise 9

Obtain books on model making from the library. Look for and list ideas which you think could be used for coursework. Add them to your resource bank.

You might like carrying out a survey

Surveys about people, places and things.

Social surveys

A social survey uses questionnaires or interviews to collect information about people.

Example. How much pocket money do pupils in your school receive each week? Using a short questionnaire, you could find out the amount of pocket money received by pupils according to their age and gender. Your results could be presented in various ways, e.g. bar charts and pie charts. You can show statistically the connection between age, gender and amount of pocket money.

Traffic surveys

A traffic survey involves counting the number and types of vehicle at one or more places at various times and dates.

Example. You could survey the different types of vehicle passing your school entrance at close of morning school. Do this every day for a week. By statistical analysis you can show the connection between volume and type of traffic, and perhaps determine how dangerous it is to rush out of school.

Land surveys

A land survey examines the boundaries, shape, location and contours of land and /or buildings.

Example. You could obtain a book on surveying from the library. Make some simple surveying instruments – a plane-table is very easy to make. You may like to survey your school and school playing area. This task will require a sound knowledge of geometry, trigonometry and bearings as well as scale drawing, ratio and proportion.

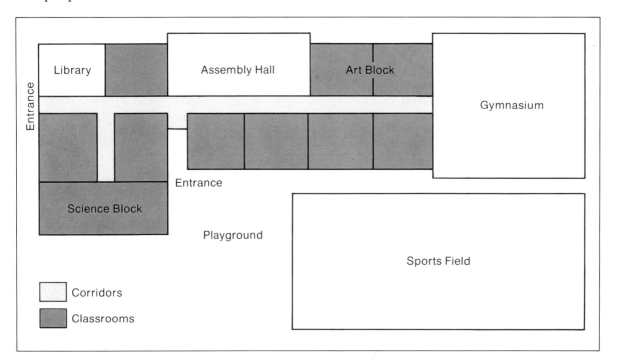

Exercise 10

1. List three ideas for social surveys which could be conducted using a sample of pupils from your own school.
2. List three examples of a social survey which could be conducted using a sample of parents of pupils from your own school.

You might like organising an event

A sports event

Example. If you were to organise the school table tennis tournament it would be necessary to arrange knock-out matches to ensure that you finish with your two finalists. You could measure the hall to see how many tables can be used at any one time. You could cost the tournament, ensuring that entrance fees cover the cost of equipment and prizes. You could consider the percentage of pupils taking part, and the ratio of boys to girls.

A fund raising event

Example. You may like to organise a sponsored activity for charity (or the school fund). This could involve the measurement of time and distance (e.g. for a sponsored run) and the collection of money.

A social event

Example. You could organise a school trip for your end of term outing. As well as costing the trip, fare, food, etc., you will need to collect and read bus and train timetables and to make a decision on the best, quickest and cheapest way to travel.

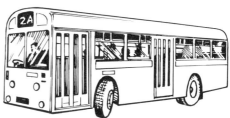

Exercise 11

Work in a group and make a list of as many social events as you can that could be used for a coursework assignment. Choose three and show how they involve mathematics.

You might like carrying out an experiment

The work you do in Science provides an excellent source for experiments that could be used for coursework in Mathematics.

Investigations

Example 1. You could make a collection of containers of different body widths and neck lengths (bottles, cans, etc.). Fill each of them with water, 50cc at a time, and measure the height of the water after each addition. Draw a graph of height against volume with a scale drawing of each container alongside its own graph. The results could then be developed further, comparing different containers and even predicting the shape of the graph that would result from a particular container shape.

Example 2. You could investigate pattern in a random event, e.g. tossing coins, throwing dice. There is no pattern in a single random event, consequently the coursework will involve observing a large number of similar events and the recording of each outcome. This will lead to frequency tables, histograms and will involve ratio, proportion and probability.

Building a model

Example. You may like to build an experimental model. You could design and build a model crane. This will involve measurement of mass, length, volume, and may include some trigonometry and work on structures.

Exercise 12

What areas of mathematics will be involved in an experiment to compare the extension of a length of wire with the weight suspended from it? State briefly how you could extend this as a piece of coursework.

Part 2 Choosing an idea

You should by now have lots of different ideas for coursework tasks in your resource bank but what do you do with them?

What shall I do?

◄ **Choose something which appeals to you.** You will work much harder if you are interested in what you are doing.

Star Wars, lasers, quasars!!

Choose something which you feel you can cope with. Some of your ideas and thoughts may seem exciting at first . . . but you may find it difficult to extend or develop them. ▶

Mathematics around the world . . . Hm!

◄ **Choose a topic that you can easily investigate**. Focus your attention on a specific area. This will make it easier to collect information.

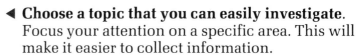

How would I get to Mars?

Choose something that it is possible to find out about. Planning 'a new town' may seem very exciting, but designing a garden shed is much more realistic. Planners of new towns take years to research their ideas . . . you could get a catalogue of garden sheds tomorrow! ▶

I know, I will choose my hobby!

◀ **Choose a topic you know something about.**
It will make it easier to plan your work and give
you confidence in your results.

Does your teacher approve?

This is important because your coursework could be part of a GCSE assessment
and the teacher will know whether your intended task will be acceptable to the
examining board. Use your teacher as a **resource** to help you to 'cut corners' –
don't turn your coursework into an endurance test.

Part 3 Getting going

Having chosen the idea for your coursework you now need to develop that idea.
Here are some suggestions which should help you.

Planning a holiday

You might choose to plan a holiday, so how do you get started? One way is to
'brainstorm' ideas, that is, simply make a list of things that you think are relevant as
they come to mind. They can be organised, changed or rejected later.

I want to plan a summer holiday.

Questions to ask

Where to? . . . home or abroad . . .
What type of holiday? . . . sport . . . lazing in the sun . . .
Travel? . . . coach . . . plane . . . boat . . .
Accommodation? . . . full board . . . half board . . . self catering . . .
Cost? . . . fixed budget . . . money no object . . .

Exercise 1
List some more questions that are relevant to planning a holiday.

You can now consider these questions in detail, for example:

● What type of holiday?

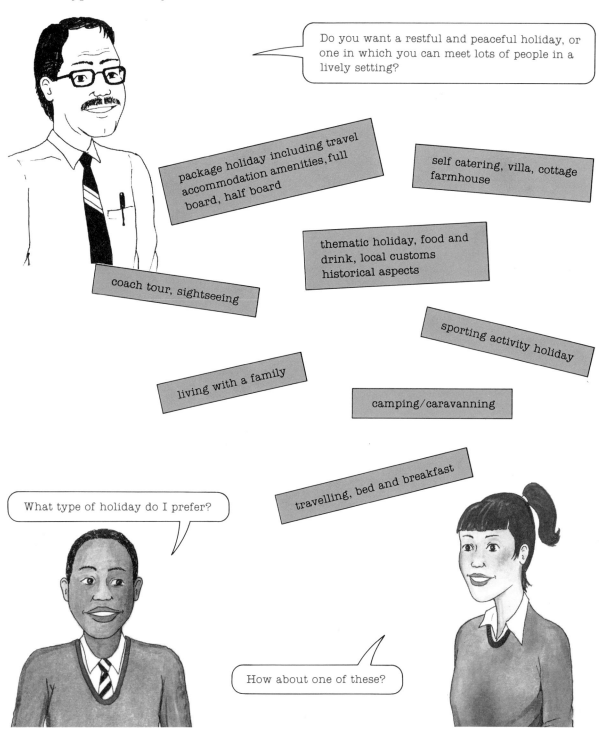

Do you want a restful and peaceful holiday, or one in which you can meet lots of people in a lively setting?

package holiday including travel accommodation amenities, full board, half board

self catering, villa, cottage farmhouse

thematic holiday, food and drink, local customs historical aspects

coach tour, sightseeing

sporting activity holiday

living with a family

camping/caravanning

travelling, bed and breakfast

What type of holiday do I prefer?

How about one of these?

Let's choose 'travelling, bed and breakfast'.

Here are some questions which you would need to consider:

- What method of transport will you be using?
- How far do you want to travel?
- How many nights will you want to stay in each place?
- Do you have to book your accommodation in advance?
- What time do you have to vacate the accommodation?

Exercise 2

Add to the above list any other questions you need to consider for a bed and breakfast holiday.

Exercise 3

Imagine you choose a thematic holiday, that is a holiday designed for people who wish to pursue a particular interest, e.g. history, language, literature, wine, local customs.

Write down questions you would ask to help you get going with your planning.

Exercise 4

Brainstorm the planning of a day's sightseeing trip. (This would be easier to do if you worked as a member of a group.)

Designing an object

Let's say you decided to design and build a dog kennel as your coursework task. What sort of questions should you ask to get going?

Questions to ask

What is a suitable and practical dog kennel?
How big should it be?
What materials should I use?
How much will it cost?
Should it be fixed or portable?

I would like to make a kennel for my dog

Now consider these questions in more detail, for example:

● How big should it be?

The kennel must be big enough for the dog!

Can he turn round?
Will he grow any more?
Is the entrance large enough for him to get in and out?

● How much will it cost?

What sort of things will affect the cost?

- flat roof or slanted roof
- floor or no floor
- door or no door

- how long you want the kennel to last
- the strength of the kennel so it won't fall apart.

- weatherproofing so it won't rot
- wanting to keep the dog dry and warm.

- using materials that are easily available and don't cost too much.

You may find this type of task will also be useful for a C. D. T. project.

Exercise 5

Suppose you were designing a bread bin. Make a list of the questions you would ask to help you get going with your planning.

Developing your idea

You have now looked at two examples of developing an idea for coursework. They contain a number of techniques which you will find useful.

- **Brainstorming** – making a list of anything and everything you can think of connected with the topic.
- **Questioning** – asking a series of questions which are relevant to the topic.
- **Imagining** – using your imagination to picture a situation, an event or an object.

Conducting an investigation

The coursework task that you choose may be an investigation. Before you can get started make sure you understand the problem.

Read this carefully and think about what you would do

CROSSES 1

Here are the first three shapes in a sequence of crosses.

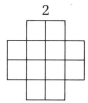
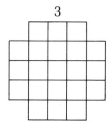

Can you explain how you could work out the area and perimeter of bigger crosses ... (say the 100th or 200th cross in sequence) ... **without drawing them?**

Don't be afraid to **explore** the problem.
Go on, have a go!

Did you get stuck!
Don't worry, this is quite normal.
There is usually a way out.

You may well have picked crosses at random, but
that is not really a good plan.

Here are a number of strategies you could try:

- Build the crosses up step by step using multilink cubes, or squares cut from card.
- Draw/build the next few crosses in the sequence.
- Look for any patterns as the crosses grow.
  (Remember, patterns can occur in number, measurement and shape.)
- Is there a method which will help you to work out the area and perimeter quickly?

We are not going to go through all these
strategies fully. As an example we will explore
one of these suggestions. This investigation is
considered in more detail in a later section.

STARTING YOUR ASSIGNMENT

Looking for a pattern

Here are **three** different ways in which you might visualise cross 3 page 29 being split up in order to find its area.

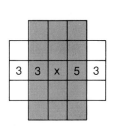

$$3 + (3 \times 5) + 3 =$$

21 sq. units

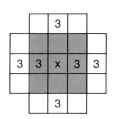

$$3 + 3 + (3 \times 3) + 3 + 3 =$$

21 sq. units

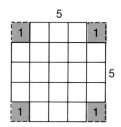

$$(5 \times 5) - 4 =$$

21 sq. units

All give the same area!

You should now be able to see ways in which you could visualise the perimeters.

Exercise 6

Look again at the pattern of crosses as they grow and look for any patterns in the perimeters.

Draw some diagrams to show different ways in which you might visualise cross 3 being split up in order to find the perimeter.

Developing an investigation

To successfully begin an investigation you need to develop a strategy. A strategy in this sense is a plan or approach designed to see what happens if a particular course of action is taken. It may be that certain changes may make a difference or that there is more than one approach. Try to develop a number of strategies and choose the one you think is the best.

Conducting an experiment

Your coursework in mathematics might include experimental work. Suppose you decide to study how a pendulum on a clock works. What sort of questions should you ask to get going?

What does grandad do to the pendulum on his clock to make it go faster or slower?

Questions to ask

Does he increase the weight on the pendulum?
Does he alter the starting angle of the pendulum?
Does he alter the length of the pendulum?

Exercise 7

Does he increase the weight on the pendulum?
Write down what observations you would need to make in order to answer this question.

Developing an experiment

To develop an experiment as a piece of coursework make sure you:

- understand what you are doing,
- have the equipment you need,
- know what data you require,
- make careful observations,
- record your results accurately.

Exercise 8

This section has dealt with the development of ideas for coursework. A key part of this process is the asking of questions.

Choose an activity from your resource bank. Generate some questions to help you to get going on this activity.

Here is a summary of the **key strategies** for getting going on your assignment task.

Enjoy it!

- Make sure you understand the task.
- Ask relevant questions.
- Try some particular cases.
- Know what results you need to record.
- Draw helpful diagrams.
- Know what equipment you need.
- Simplify difficult tasks.
- Don't be afraid to try things out, even if you're not sure where they are leading.
- Look for patterns.

SECTION C

Part 1 What data do I need?

This section deals with how to collect data. It begins with the steps you need to take **before** you collect or generate data. It makes more sense to talk about **how** to collect data when you know **what** you are collecting and **why** you are collecting it.

Planning a holiday

In planning a holiday let's look at **what sort of data** to collect and **why** it is needed.

Imagine that you are planning a skiing holiday abroad, for a man, his wife and two teenage children.

Below are listed different items of data required to plan a skiing holiday, with reasons for collecting them. They have been grouped into different types of data to make the planning easier and more systematic.

Data to collect	Reasons why
● Equipment – What specialist equipment or clothing is needed? – Person's height. – Shoe size.	So that you can be safe, comfortable and properly equipped for the sport. Budget for this in your spending. For the length of the skis. To make sure your boots fit and are waiting for you on arrival.

Data to collect	Reasons why
● Costing	
– Prices for different times of the year.	Cost varies.
– Comparative cost of holiday in different countries.	Cost varies.
– Discount for children/groups.	May affect the holiday you choose.
– How much spending money?	The cost of living may be different in a foreign country than in the UK. You may have to pay for ski instruction. You may have to pay for medical treatment.
– Can you buy foreign currency in the UK or do you wait until you get there?	For convenience or there may be currency restrictions.
– Cash or traveller's cheques.	For security.
– Dates of school holidays.	So that the children can go on holiday without missing school.
– Snow guarantee.	Some travel companies will compensate you for not being able to ski due to lack of snow.
– Travel insurance	For adequate sickness and injury cover.
● Resort	
– Resort height	For likelihood of snow for early or late holidays.
– Variety of ski runs	For different levels of skiing expertise.
– Transfer time from airport to resort.	To minimise travelling time.
– Apres-ski entertainment.	If you can't ski because of injury or lack of snow.
– How far is it from the hotel to the slopes?	To cut down walking in heavy uncomfortable ski boots carrying unmanageable skis.
● Country	
– What type of passport?	A 1 year Visitors' Passport may not be sufficient.
– Do you need a visa?	Some countries require special permission for entry.

Data to collect	Reasons why
● **Ski Instruction**	
– Previous skiing experience.	To be placed in a suitable ski-class.
– Do the instructors speak English?	For clear and safe instruction, especially for beginners.
– Number of hours ski instruction per day.	For value for money and sufficient time to learn and enjoy skiing.

Exercise 1

Choose one of the following groups of people and imagine you are planning a holiday for them.

1. A man, his wife and two children aged 7 years and 10 years who plan to take a camping holiday in France.
2. A retired couple who like the weather warm, but not too hot, and plan to have a holiday touring by coach.
3. Three young people ages 21, 22 and 23, who decide to spend all their savings on a sailing holiday abroad.

List the data you need to collect and the reasons why you require this information.

Exercise 2

List the data you need to collect and the reasons you need it before you can begin to build a dog kennel. This involves planning of a different kind. (The exercise on page 27 contains a number of suggestions which will help you with your answer.)

Now apply what you have learned so far about collecting data to the following exercise.

Exercise 3

Describe what data you would need to collect in order to design and build a computer desk and state why you need this information.

A problem or investigation

When solving a problem or exploring an investigation you need to consider **what sort of data** is required at each stage.

If you were tackling an investigation like 'Crosses 1' (page 29) you should consider:

– what data you have at the **start of the task**
– what **new data** you need to explore the problem
– what **further data** you need in order to discover any patterns or to solve the problem.

Let's look at these in turn

1. The data you **start with** are the first three shapes in a sequence of crosses as shown below.

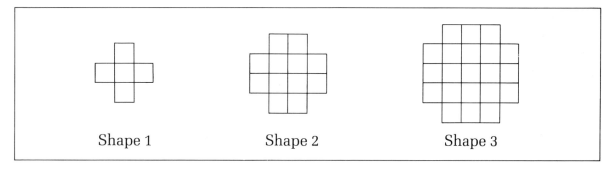

Shape 1   Shape 2   Shape 3

2. The **new data** you need to explore the problem would be obtained by building or drawing some more crosses in the sequence.

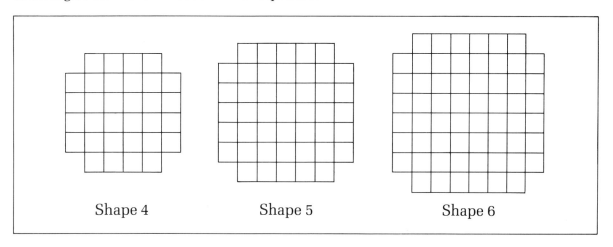

Shape 4   Shape 5   Shape 6

3. The **further data** you need to discover a pattern would be obtained by examining the area and perimeter of each cross.

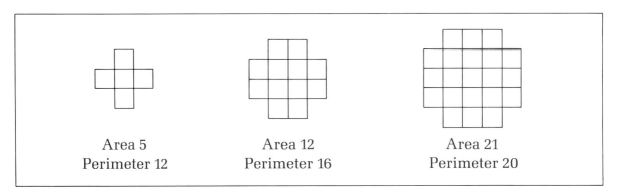

| Area 5 | Area 12 | Area 21 |
| Perimeter 12 | Perimeter 16 | Perimeter 20 |

Exercise 4

Look at the following investigation. State what data you have to start with and what further data you need to solve the problem.

MATCHES

How may matchsticks are required if you have 14 squares in a row? The side of each square is the length of one match as shown in this part of the sequence.

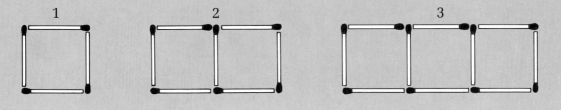

When trying to decide **what data** is needed, it is useful to consider the different forms of data you can collect.

1. **Statistical data** obtained from questionnaires and surveys.

Example. You could make a survey of the different types of vehicle passing your school at a certain time of day.

2. **Experimental data** collected through practical work.

Example. Observing the change in length of a piece of wire as increasing weights are suspended from it.

3. **Generated data** gathered from investigational or problem-solving activities.

Example. Investigating the relationship between the number of faces, edges and vertices of different solid figures.

Exercise 5

Give one example of a task which would require you to collect:

1. Statistical data
2. Experimental data
3. Generated data

You need to know **what** data or information to collect and **why** you require that data. Here are some questions to ask.

- What do I already **know**?
- What do I **want**?
- **Why** do I need it?

Part 2 How to collect data

Collecting information is a major part of any assignment task and needs to be planned carefully. Having decided what you are looking for, you now have to decide how to collect it.

Here are some points to consider.

There are two sources of information.

1. **Primary sources** – this is information which you have **generated** yourself. You may obtain this information by:

   – conducting an experiment
   – using a questionnaire
   – conducting an interview
   – making an investigation.

2. **Secondary sources** – this is **existing** data that has been collected and recorded by someone else.

You may obtain this information from:

  – official statistics – the town hall
  – the media – newspapers, TV
  – reference books – the public library
  – holiday brochures – travel agents
  – textbooks – your teachers.

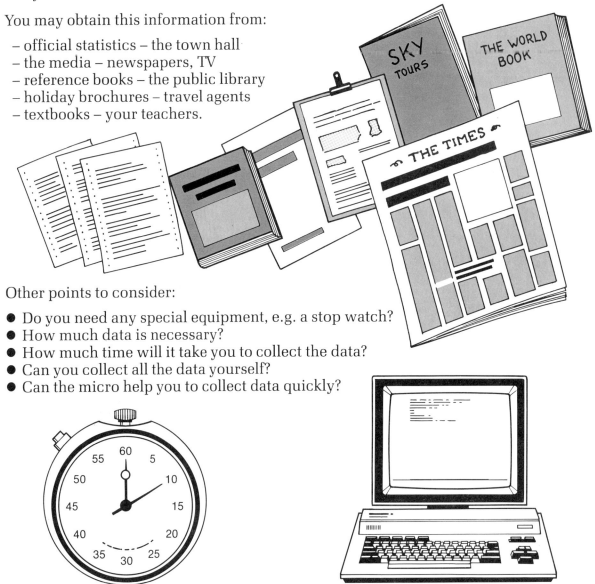

Other points to consider:

● Do you need any special equipment, e.g. a stop watch?
● How much data is necessary?
● How much time will it take you to collect the data?
● Can you collect all the data yourself?
● Can the micro help you to collect data quickly?

The information needed will decide the way in which it is collected. In many tasks you may need to use both primary and secondary sources of information.

You might decide that you would like to:

  – organise an event
  – investigate a number pattern
  – do a simple experiment
  – carry out a survey.

Organising an event

If you are planning a skiing holiday (page 34) you will need to collect data from existing sources and you will need to generate some data of your own.

- Visit several travel agents to obtain brochures.
- Visit local sport shops to price equipment.
- Check the rate of exchange at the bank.

This data already exists.

- Ask the members of your party their height and shoe sizes.

This is data you are generating yourself.

> **Exercise 1**
> Turn to Section B page 21 and make a list of the ways of collecting the data required to organise a school trip. State whether it is primary or secondary data.

If you are organising an event.

- Decide what data you need.
- Where it can be collected.
- How it can be collected.
- Can you collect it yourself or do you need help?

SECTION C

Investigating a number pattern

To investigate what happens if you add a pair of consecutive triangle numbers in sequence.

1. **Consider the data you have**

I want to study triangle numbers.

Questions to ask

What are triangle numbers?
How does the sequence build up?

Consider how the red balls are arranged on a snooker table.

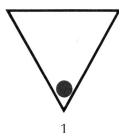      

This arrangement shows how triangle numbers are formed.

1   1 + 2 = 3   1 + 2 + 3 = 6

You can show triangular numbers as a triangular pattern of dots, and so build up an information table

	1st	2nd	3rd	4th	5th
Triangle numbers	1	3	6	10	15

What happens if I add a pair of consecutive triangle numbers?

2. Generate new data to get going

Continue the table of triangle numbers up to the tenth number.
Add together the first two triangle numbers.
1 and 3.
Add the 2nd and 3rd triangle numbers, 3 and 6.
Draw diagrams to help.

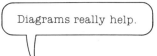

Diagrams really help.

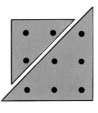

$1 + 3 = 4$ $3 + 6 = 9$

Now add the 3rd and 4th triangle numbers
and the 4th and 5th triangle numbers.
Again draw diagrams to help.

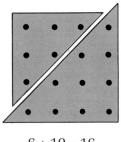

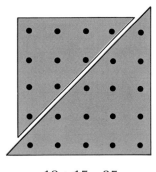

$6 + 10 = 16$ $10 + 15 = 25$

3. **Generate further data to look for a pattern**

Make a table to show the numbers formed by adding consecutive triangle numbers up to the 9th and 10th triangle number.

Position of triangle number	Triangle numbers	Result
1st + 2nd	1 + 3	4
2nd + 3rd	3 + 6	
3rd + 4th		
9th + 10th		

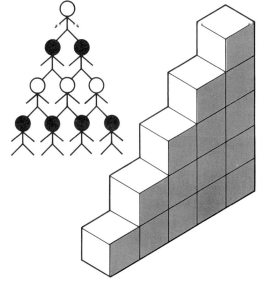

When doing an investigation.

- Break the problem into simpler units.
- Decide what information you have.
- Generate new data by continuing the sequence to several places.
- Draw diagrams if they help.
- Generate further data and look for links between elements of the sequence.
- Ask questions like
  – What will happen if – I **change** this, I **do** this, I **swap** these, I **remove** this?
  – If I turn this diagram around will things become clearer?
  – Will this diagram split up into simpler parts?

Conducting an experiment

This example shows how to generate your own data by doing an experiment and **observing** the results. Experiments set out to discover the effect of one thing on another. You will have done experiments in your science lessons.

Suppose you are studying the swing of a pendulum. You may decide to produce a set of results by recording the effect that changing the length of the pendulum has on the time of the swing.

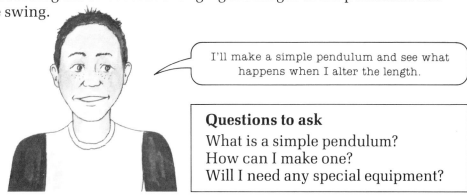

I'll make a simple pendulum and see what happens when I alter the length.

Questions to ask
What is a simple pendulum?
How can I make one?
Will I need any special equipment?

A simple pendulum is just a small weight suspended from a piece of thread. You can make one quite easily. Use a small metal nut for the weight and a strong piece of thread. You will need a stop watch to time the swing.

1. Attach the pendulum to a suitable point and practise counting and timing swings in order to be as accurate as possible.

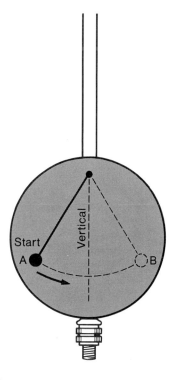

2. To collect the data, observe the time taken for 20 complete swings of the pendulum. Alter the length of the thread and repeat the experiment several times. You could record your results in a table.

Length of pendulum (in cm)	0	10	20	30	40	100
Time for 20 swings (in secs)	0					

Exercise 2

Design an experiment to find the relationship between the circumference and diameter of any circle. Describe the data you need to collect and how you would record that data.

When conducting an experiment

Before starting your experiment

- Think about what you are trying to find out.
- Plan and prepare your experiment:
    - collect the equipment you need
    - decide what data you need to collect
    - decide how you will record your results.

Carrying out your experiment

- Make careful observations as you go along.
- Record your results as they happen.

Carrying out a Survey

I would like to do a survey.

Questions to ask

What sort of survey? . . . music . . . sport . . . pet food
Who should I ask? . . . pupils . . . teachers . . . the public
How many people? . . . all . . . a few . . . a sample
How can I obtain my information? . . . questionnaire . . .
interview

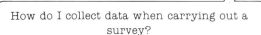

How do I collect data when carrying out a
survey?

Questionnaires

Surveys are often based on questionnaires. In its broadest sense a questionnaire is
simply a list of questions.

There are two ways of presenting questions.

1. The questions can be read to the person taking part by an interviewer who may
    tick or write down the answers. This is known as a structured interview.
2. The questions may be written down and copies of the questionnaire taken or
    posted to the participants who then write down their answers and return them.

To choose which to use you should consider the advantages and disadvantages of each method.

	Advantages	Disadvantages
Questionnaire	● A large number of people can be questioned. ● The person has time to think about their answers.	● Possibility of not getting many questionnaires back. ● You cannot explain the questions to the person.
Structured interview	● The interviewer can explain the questions and give more detail if needed. ● Many questions can be asked quickly and a high response rate can be achieved.	● The manner and appearance of the interviewer can affect answers. For example, by asking leading questions and so creating bias. ● Time consuming, you may not be given enough time out of school.

Exercise 3

In each of the following situations advise the researcher on whether to use a questionnaire or a structured interview. Give reasons for your advice.

1. I need to ask as many people as possible which brand of coffee they prefer.
2. I want to know if the pupils of my school think they need more mathematics lessons and if so how many more – and I require thoughtful answers.
3. I want to know which sport is the most popular in school.
4. I need to know the **exact** age of the person answering my questions about leisure time activities.

How do I construct a questionnaire?

This is what you should be trying to do.

You should:

- Work out exactly what you want to find out and only use questions which will help you achieve this.
- Explain the purpose behind the questionnaire and stress that the answers are confidential.
- Ask questions which are clear, simple and unambiguous.
- Be as brief as possible.

Avoid doing this.

You should not:

- Ask questions which are impossible to answer.
- Be sexist, racist or cause offence.
- Use leading questions, e.g. You probably agree, don't you, that . . .
- Use vague descriptive words, e.g. Do you prefer long or short stories? What is 'long' for one person may be 'short' for someone else!

Take note of this.

It is important to remember that even if all your questions are clear, brief and easy to answer the whole questionnaire should be as short as possible. Long questionnaires tend to be answered badly as people tire of them.

Exercise 4

State briefly what you think is wrong with the following questions.

1. What is your opinion of the Seychelles as a holiday resort?
   (Tick one box) excellent ☐ fair ☐ poor ☐
2. Does your husband help with the housework?   Yes/No
3. Inflation moves inexorably upwards. Briefly comment on this statement
4. I assume you prefer beer to lager. Correct? Yes/No

More about questions

Questions can be grouped into two types **closed** and **open**.

Closed questions are usually easy to answer as a person simply has to choose between alternatives that are presented to them.

Example.

> How do you travel to school? (Tick the appropriate box)
>
> CAR ☐   WALK ☐   CYCLE ☐   BUS ☑   TRAIN ☐   TAXI ☐

Open questions allow people to give the answers they want. This might not be possible with closed questions which force them to choose between alternatives that you have decided upon.

Example.

> How do you travel to school, and why do you travel that way?
>
> I go to school on the bus because my mum won't let me use my bike in case it gets stolen from the playground. If we had proper bike sheds I could use my bike. Mind you sometimes I don't mind walking when the weather is nice but I would still come on the bus if it is raining a lot.

By looking at the two examples given you can see that the way in which a person is allowed to answer may affect greatly the type of data you will receive. Most questionnaires contain both closed and open questions because researchers will need both specific information – facts and figures – and peoples' views and opinions.

Consider the next point very carefully!

If the main purpose of your questionnaire is to produce statistics which can be represented by charts and graphs then you should use **closed** questions. They produce answers which can be easily counted and analysed.

Here is an example of a questionnaire designed to discover the eating habits at breakfast, of pupils in a school. It aims to obtain data in order to investigate possible connections between pupils' age, gender and what they have for breakfast.

Questionnaire

I am doing a survey to discover what pupils eat and drink for breakfast. Would you please help me by answering the following questions?

Age .... years .... months

Place a tick in the box (boxes) which apply to you.

Q1. Gender   Male   ☐ 1   Female   ☐ 2

Q2. Do you eat: Cornflakes   ☐ 1   Weetabix   ☐ 5
                    Rice Krispies   ☐ 2   muesli   ☐ 6
                    porridge   ☐ 3   bacon   ☐ 7
                    eggs   ☐ 4   toast   ☐ 8
                    others (please state)............................... 9

Q3. Do you drink: orange juice   ☐ 1   apple juice ☐ 4
                     grapefruit juice ☐ 2   milk   ☐ 5
                     tea   ☐ 3   coffee   ☐ 6
                     others (please state)............................... 7

Q4. Do you think you have a nutritious breakfast?
Give reasons for your answer..
....
....

Q5. If your answer to question 4 is no, briefly state why you do not have an adequate breakfast..
....

Exercise 5

In view of the aims of the research:

1. Are there sufficient questions on the questionnaire?
   Give reasons for your answer. If you think additional questions are required, write them down.
2. Are the questions phrased adequately? Give reasons for your answer. If you think they can be improved, replace the questions.

Exercise 6

You decide to carry out a survey into the sporting interests of pupils aged 11 to 18 years at your school.

Your survey should include sports that the pupils take part in and also the sport they watch (either live or on TV).

Your aim is to investigate how the **time** spent on these interests varies according to the **age** and **gender** of the pupils, e.g. do girls play more sport than boys?

Design a suitable questionnaire for obtaining the information you would need to carry out the survey.

Once you have designed your questionnaire you need to decide who is going to answer it.

It is not usually possible to give questionnaires to every person in the 'population' you are interested in, whether that 'population' is the pupils in your school, those living on a local estate, or the whole of Great Britain! This means that you will have to choose a smaller number of people to study. This smaller number is called your **sample**.

What size should my sample be?

Your sample should not be so large that it is impossible to collect data from everyone in it, but large enough to accurately **represent** the population. A sample of 10 out of a population of 1000 is very unlikely to be **representative**, however carefully it is chosen!

A **representative sample** is one in which the results obtained from the sample can be taken to be true for the whole population.

Example. If 40% of a representative sample smoke cigarettes then we can say that it is likely that 40% of the population smoke cigarettes.

Choosing a representative sample

Here are four different ways of choosing a representative sample.

Random Sampling

Choosing at random does not mean choosing 'any old how', but choosing as in a raffle. Give every member of the population a number and then pick numbers from a hat. For large populations the numbers are not taken from a hat but are taken from tables of random numbers or are created by a random number generating machine, e.g. a computer.

Systematic Sampling

As its name suggests this method uses a system. The system in this case involves regularity. Begin with a list of people and choose every third, fourth or whatever member on the list.

Stratified Sampling

If you *know* that your population can be divided into two or more different groups, your sample should include people in the same proportion as the numbers in each group. For example, if you wanted to estimate the average weight of all the people over 18 years of age living in Britain and you *know* that 45% of the population are male and 55% are female then your sample should contain 45% males and 55% females. You could then take a random or a systematic sample from each group.

Quota Sampling

In a quota sample you are not given the names of people to interview. Instead you would interview different groups of people. For example you may be told to interview as many men as women, or maybe twenty adults and ten children. In a school survey you may be told to interview any thirty first year pupils, twenty second year pupils and so on.

Care must be taken in selecting your sample. If you used the questionnaire on page 52 to obtain views of a sample of pupils in your school it would be no use asking only first year pupils. This would create a **bias** towards the first year and may not reflect the opinion of the total 'population'.

> So we need to be sure that our sample is representative

Exercise 7

You have decided to use the questionnaire from Exercise 6 to obtain the views of a sample of pupils at a High School.

The School consists of 1000 pupils, 200 in each of the first and second years, 150 in each of the third, fourth and fifth years, and 75 in each of the sixth and seventh years.

Describe briefly how you would select a sample of 120 pupils by:

1. Random sampling
2. Stratified sampling
3. Quota sampling.

You should now know all about questionnaires.

Before using a questionnaire:

- Know what you are trying to find out.
- Take great care in the wording of your questions and in the instructions to the user.
- Try a dummy run (pilot study) to test whether your questions are clear and relevant.
- Choose your sample carefully.
- Think about the number of copies you need.
- Tell the people completing the questionnaire who you are, what you are doing and that their answers are confidential.
- Make careful arrangements for the collection of the questionnaires.
- Think about what you are going to do with your results.

Now you know how to collect data.

- Decide **what** data you want to collect.

- Decide **why** you want that data.

- Decide **how** you will collect the data:
    - when organising an event explore all sources of data.
    - when conducting an investigation, look at the given data and decide what further data you need to generate.
    - when doing an experiment make careful observations.
    - when conducting a survey use a questionnaire or carry out an interview.

- Remember there are both **primary** and **secondary** sources of data.

SECTION D

Once you have collected your data you will need to consider how to represent it. Clear and accurate presentation of your findings is an important part of coursework.

> There are several ways to present your information.

- in words
- in symbols
- in tables
- in charts
- in graphs
- in diagrams
- in working models

The type of data you have collected will influence the way in which that data is presented. You should choose the most appropriate method or combination of methods to display your findings.

Tables and Charts

Example. You may conduct a survey of 90 pupils in your year to discover how they travel to school. You could represent your findings in the following ways.

1. A frequency table

A frequency table shows how often each item occurs. **'Tallying'** is useful when counting things.

Method	Tally (count)	Frequency (f)
Train	|||||	5
Bus	||||| ||||| ||	12
Walk	||||| ||||| ||||| ||||| ||||| ||||| ||||| ||||| ||||| |||||	50
Cycle	||||| ||||| ||||| ||	17
Car	|||||		6
	Total	90

2. A chart

This could be a pictogram, pie chart, or bar chart.

● **Pictograms**. A pictogram is a chart which uses symbols or pictures to show information.

A pictogram to show how pupils travel to school

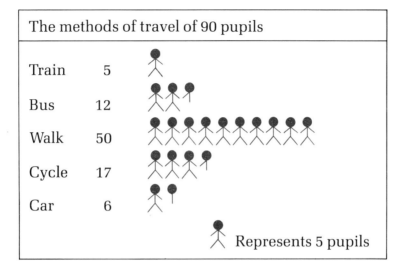

The methods of travel of 90 pupils		
Train	5	
Bus	12	
Walk	50	
Cycle	17	
Car	6	

Represents 5 pupils

Unless you are spending time on a special project do not draw elaborate symbols. If you use a pictogram you must make clear what your symbol represents. Notice the 'part' symbols, (only the straight lines count as a 'part').

Do not forget...
Make it easy to understand.
Keep the symbols simple.

● **Pie charts.** Pie charts are circles which are cut up into 'slices' to show the different parts which make up the whole. The angles at the centre of the circle are proportional to the number each 'slice' represents.

A pie chart to show how pupils travel to school

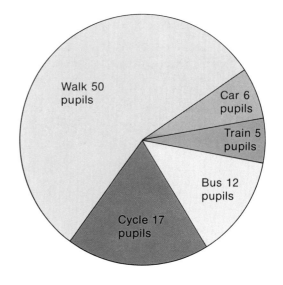

Since 90 pupils are represented by 360°
1 pupil is represented by 4°
Train   5 × 4° = 20°
Bus   12 × 4° = 48°
Walk   50 × 4° = 200°
Cycle   17 × 4° = 68°
Car   6 × 4° = 24°

(It is not necessary to mark the sizes of angles on the diagram if you show your working clearly as above. The diagram shows the statistical figures and is clearer without the angle markings.)

You've all seen these types of charts before

● **Bar charts** These use rows or columns to show how often certain things occur.

Method of travel of 90 pupils

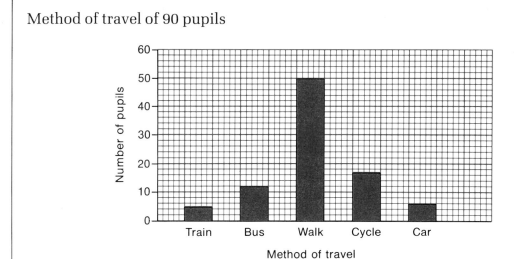

(The rectangles should all have the same width.)

Bar charts could be *horizontal* instead of *vertical*

Method of travel of 90 pupils

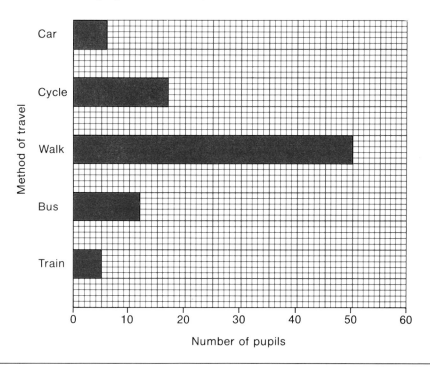

Statistical diagrams should have headings to describe them. Scales should be clearly marked. Axes should be labelled.

Exercise 1

This frequency table shows the breakfast drink of 30 pupils in a second year class.
Draw a pictogram and a bar chart to represent this data.

drink	tally	frequency
orange	l	1
tea	l#l l#l l#l	15
coffee	l#l ll	7
milk	llll	4
cocoa	ll	2
grapefruit	l	1
total		30

Exercise 2

Find out what you can about other types of bar charts. Illustrate your answer with examples from newspapers or magazines.

How many more types of bar chart are there?

Hm . . . these sound interesting.

Comparative Bar Chart
Composite Bar Chart
Percentage Bar Chart
Comp......

Exercise 3

The following table shows the goals for and against the first ten teams in the English First Division in Season 1987/88. Draw a compound bar chart to represent the given data.

	For	Against
Liverpool	87	24
Manchester United	71	38
Nottingham Forest	67	39
Everton	53	27
QPR	48	38
Arsenal	48	39
Wimbledon	58	47
Newcastle	55	53
Luton	57	58
Coventry	46	53

Exercise 4

The following table shows the average daily maximum hours of sunshine in Majorca between April and October. It also compares the maximum temperature in °F with that in London for the same period.

APR	MAY	JUN	JUL	AUG	SEP	OCT
Average daily max. hours of sun						
7	9	10	11	10	8	·6
Average daily max. temp. °F						
66	71	78	84	83	80	72
London °F						
57	63	69	71	71	66	58

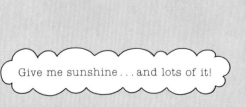

Give me sunshine ... and lots of it!

1. Draw a pictogram to show the average daily maximum hours of sunshine in Majorca.
2. Draw a comparative bar chart to represent the temperature in Majorca with that in London over the period April to October.

The main purpose of representing data with a chart is to make it easily and quickly understandable.

It is useless using pictorial representation unless it is:

- Easier to understand than the figures it represents.
- Clear in its meaning.
- Adequately labelled.

You can now constrtuct all kinds of charts... good!
But, when do you use a bar chart or a pie chart!
In fact, which chart is best for which sort of data?

A bar chart shows clearly the different frequencies. It is easy to compare them. You can see at a glance which of two similar bars is longer.

A pie chart shows more easily the fraction of the total which each item takes. A sector using more than half of the circle represents more than half of the total, a sector with a small angle represents a small part of the total, and so on. It is not so easy however, to compare sectors with each other if they are nearly the same size.

A pictogram shows information in a similar way to a bar chart, but by making attractive drawings it makes it look more interesting than a bar chart, so people are more likely to look at it.

If you make pictures of different kinds, for example, a sheep, a cow and a pig, make them of equal length or you will not be able to compare the frequencies by looking at the diagram.

For example,   not

Exercise 5

In a survey 60 people in the 14–35 age range, chosen at random, were asked . . . 'Which of the following racket sports do you play most often?' 12 said badminton, 6 said none, 24 said tennis and 18 said squash. Express these answers in:

1. A table
2. A bar chart
3. A pie chart.

Which method of representing these results do you think is the best, and why?

Histograms

A histogram is used when the range of data is wide and it can be put into convenient groups called class intervals. In a histogram, the area of the 'block' represents the frequency.

1. Equal class intervals

If all class intervals have equal width, then the heights of the columns will be in proportion to their frequencies.

Example. You may do a survey on how fast (in seconds to the nearest second) members of your school can run 200 metres. The results could be represented by a frequency table and a histogram.

Here are the times in seconds (to nearest second) for a group of 40 pupils who ran 200 metres

The grouped frequency table

Class	Tally	Frequency
time in sec		
30–34	||||	4
35–39	ⅣⅠ ||||	9
40–44	ⅣⅠ ⅣⅠ ||||	14
45–49	ⅣⅠ |||	8
50–54	ⅣⅠ	5
	Total	40

The histogram

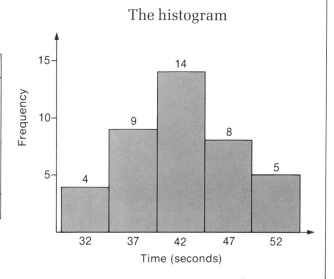

2. Unequal class intervals

A histogram can have unequal class intervals. In this case the heights of the columns must be adjusted so that the areas of the blocks are still in proportion to their frequencies.

The height of each column represents $\dfrac{\text{Frequency}}{\text{Column width}}$ and is sometimes called the frequency density.

Example. You may like to do a survey to discover the amount of pocket money received by pupils in your school. A sample of 180 pupils may produce the following results which could be represented by a table and a histogram.

The pocket money of 180 pupils

Amount (in pence)	100–139	140–159	160–169	170–179	180–199	200–259
Number of pupils (frequency)	28	24	36	38	34	20
Width of block	40	20	10	10	20	60
Freq./Width	0.7	1.2	3.6	3.8	1.7	0.33

The pocket money of 180 pupils

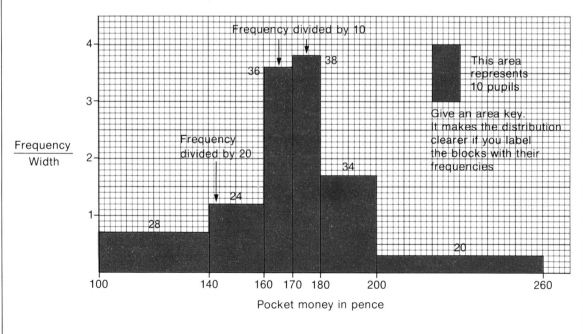

Does my task require a histogram . . . or not?

Exercise 6

In a maths exam given to 100 pupils the marks attained were collected in the following table

Marks	1–10	11–20	21–30	31–40	41–50	51–60	61–70	71–80	81–90	91–100
Frequency	5	8	10	15	20	18	10	8	4	2

Draw a histogram to represent these results.

Exercise 7

In a survey of 120 vehicles passing the school gates at lunch time, the time that elapsed between successive vehicles was collected in the following frequency table.

Class (in secs)	Tally	Frequency
0–5	ⱴ ⱴ ⱴ ∣	16
6–10	ⱴ ⱴ ∣∣∣∣	14
11–20	ⱴ ⱴ ⱴ ⱴ ⱴ	25
21–30	ⱴ ⱴ ⱴ ⱴ	20
31–40	ⱴ ⱴ ⱴ	15
41–60	ⱴ ⱴ ⱴ ∣∣∣	18
61–90	ⱴ ⱴ ∣∣	12
Total		120

Draw a histogram of the distribution

Graphs

A graph is an alternative form of pictorial representation. Every graph shows a relationship between two sets of numbers.

Example 1. You may like to do a survey of absenteeism in your school. The following figures show the number of absentees over the past ten weeks in the first year of a comprehensive school.
20, 35, 28, 25, 33, 41, 37, 46, 48, 42
They can be represented on a graph, putting time on the horizontal axis and absentees on the vertical axis.

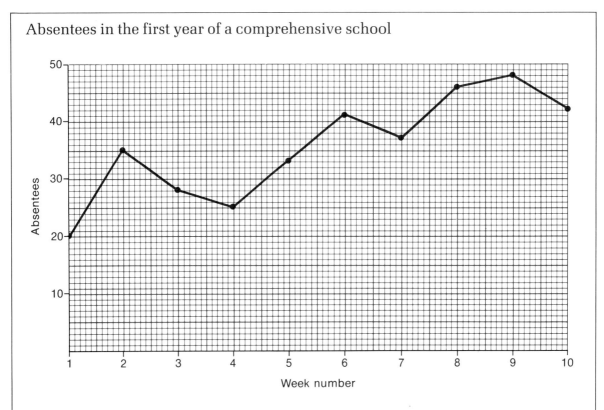

Absentees in the first year of a comprehensive school

The points are joined from one to the next by straight lines, because this shows increases and decreases more easily, but in this graph the lines have no other meaning. We cannot use the graph to find absence at in-between times, because that would be meaningless. The graph does show an upward trend in absenteeism and we might use this to make a very cautious prediction for future absence.

Example 2. In an experiment different masses were hung from the end of a piece of wire, and the extensions produced were observed and collected in the following table.

Mass (g)	50	100	150	200	250	300	350	400
Extension (cm)	1.1	1.8	2.8	4.1	5.1	5.7	7	7.8

These results may be represented by a graph. The quantity you choose (the independent variable), in this case the mass, is put along the horizontal axis. The quantity you observe (the dependent variable), in this case the extension, is put along the vertical axis.

The extension of wire suspending a given mass

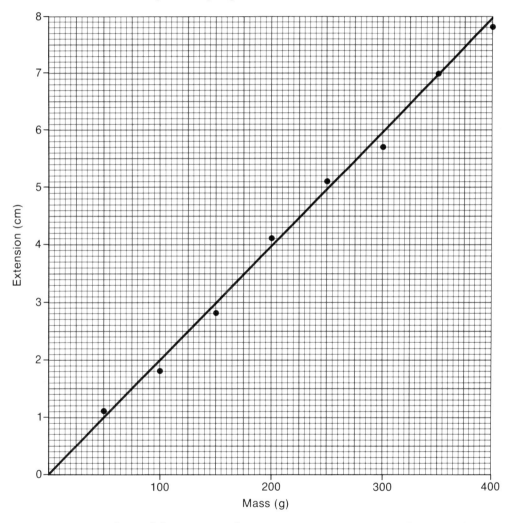

In practice, points plotted from actual measurements may not lie exactly on a straight line due to experimental errors. The **'line of best fit'** is then drawn 'through' them so that they are equally distributed about it. Any points that are well off the line stand out and may be investigated further.

Sometimes the 'line of best fit' may be a curve.

Example 3. In the pendulum experiment from page 45 you could have obtained a set of results similar to those collected in the table below.

Length of pendulum (cm)	0	10	20	30	40	50	60	70	80	90	100
Time for 20 swings (sec)	0	12.7	17.9	22.0	25.4	28.4	31.1	33.6	35.9	38.1	40.1

This data could be represented on graph paper by a smooth curve.

The time of 20 swings of a pendulum of given length

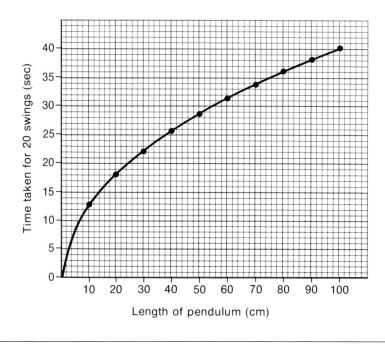

Exercise 8

The number of passengers carried by a bus company over 14 consecutive days are shown in this table.

Sun	M	Tu	W	Th	F	S	Sun	M	Tu	W	Th	F	S
10	40	30	40	48	52	24	12	40	28	35	50	52	20

Represent this data on a graph, joining each point with a straight line.

Exercise 9

Measure the circumference and radius of several different circular objects. Collect your results in a table and represent the data you collect with a graph.

Exercise 10

In an experiment to find the relationship between the area and radius of circular objects the following results were collected and recorded in a table.

r (cm)	0	1	2	3	4	5	6
A (cm2)	0	3.7	12.6	28.1	49.6	78	112

Represent this data with a graph

For all types of charts and graphs you should:

– use a title which explains what the data about is
– label axes clearly and give units.

Sometimes the data does not 'fit' a straight line or a curve. In this case a **scatter diagram** may be used. If you think there is some relationship between the two sets of variables you should again draw the '**line of best fit**' which seems to fit the **trend** of the data best. Points on one side of it should be balanced by points on the other side.

Example 4. You may like to do a survey to discover how long pupils take to travel to school. These results could be collected in a table and represented by a scatter diagram.

The distance (in Km) from school and the time (in mins) taken to travel that distance by 16 pupils are collected in the following table.

Time (min)	9	10	20	12	21	30	11	38	20	45	31	40	32	49	58	65
Distance (Km)	0.1	0.3	0.4	0.5	0.6	0.7	0.8	0.9	1	1.1	1.2	1.5	1.6	1.7	1.9	2.5

This data could be represented by the following scatter diagram.

Scatter graph relating travel time to distance

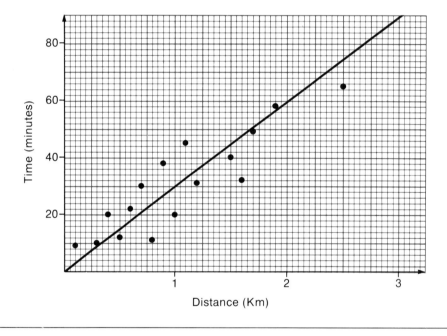

Exercise 11

The marks of 10 students in their Maths and Physics exam were:

Maths	30	36	40	43	46	50	55	60	68	70
Physics	43	42	47	49	48	53	58	58	66	88

Plot these points on a scatter diagram and draw the line of best fit. A pupil did not take his Physics but scored 45 for Maths. What mark would you give him for his Physics?

The previous examples have been concerned with ways of representing **statistical** and **experimental** data.

The examples which follow show some of the ways in which investigations and practical activities can be represented.

Diagrams

Diagrams include a variety of ways in which information can be presented. They could be number chains, networks, patterns, scale drawings and flow charts.

Number Chains

Example. A **number chain** to show how 'Happy numbers' are generated in an investigation.

32 is HAPPY   Because 32

$$3^2 \quad 2^2$$

$$9 + 4 = 13$$

$$1^2 \quad 3^2$$

$$1 + 9 = 10$$

$$1^2 \quad 0$$

$$1 + 0 = 1$$

If you end up with a 1, the number you started with is HAPPY.

Patterns

Example. Here is another diagram which shows how a **pattern** of squares can be built up to produce a snowflake design.

Start with a single square·

Starting with a single square, a complex snowflake can be built. This is what it looks like after fifteen stages.

Exercise 12

Can you discover the rule for adding coloured squares? You might like to explore these last two investigations more fully.

Networks

A **network** is a method of representing the connection between two or more points in a diagram.

Example 1. A network to show the distance in miles between 5 towns in Lincolnshire.

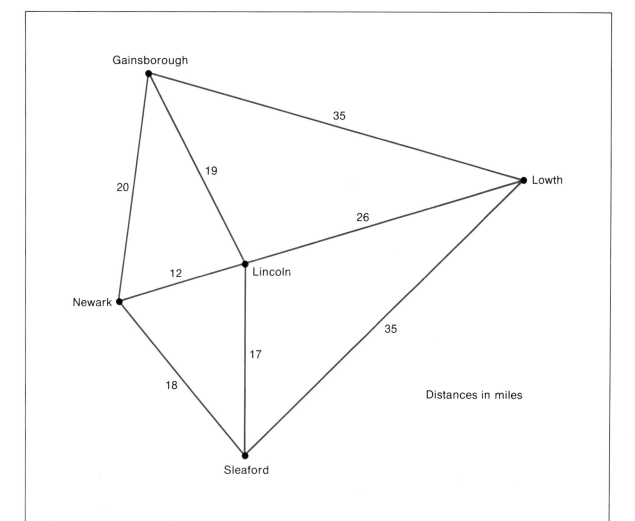

This network could be used if you wished to determine the shortest route necessary to visit all five towns.

Example 2. Route matrices, another use of a network.

If 5 places A, B, C, D, E are connected by a road system shown diagrammatically as follows, with the arrows denoting one-way roads. This could be presented in the following table

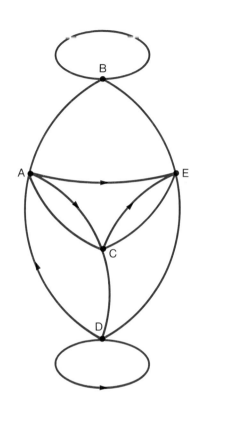

	To				
	A	B	C	D	E
A	0	1	2	0	1
B	1	2	0	0	1
From C	1	0	0	1	2
D	1	0	1	1	1
E	0	1	1	1	0

Note that the loop at B gives 2 routes from B to B because it can be travelled in both directions, but the loop at D gives only 1 route because it is one-way only.

Exercise 13

Find out from your teacher and your text book what route matrices are and how you use them.

Exercise 14

Construct a route matrix for the network shown in Example 1 above.

Flow charts

One important use of network representation is in setting out the organisation of a calculation, investigation or experiment in a **flow chart**.

Example 1. Here is a flow chart which produces chains of numbers.

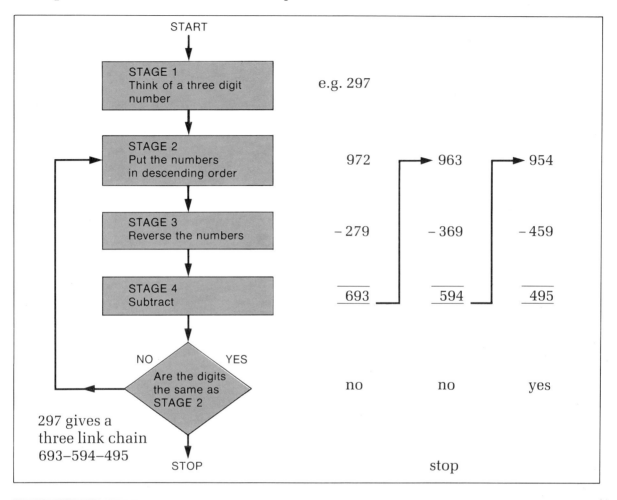

START

STAGE 1
Think of a three digit
number

e.g. 297

STAGE 2
Put the numbers
in descending order

972 → 963 → 954

STAGE 3
Reverse the numbers

− 279   − 369   − 459

STAGE 4
Subtract

693   594   495

NO   YES

Are the digits
the same as
STAGE 2

no   no   yes

297 gives a
three link chain
693−594−495

STOP   stop

Exercise 15
Draw a flow chart for Example 1, 'Happy numbers' page 73

flow charts are used a lot in computer work
aren't they?

Example 2. This flow chart tells you how to construct a cone.

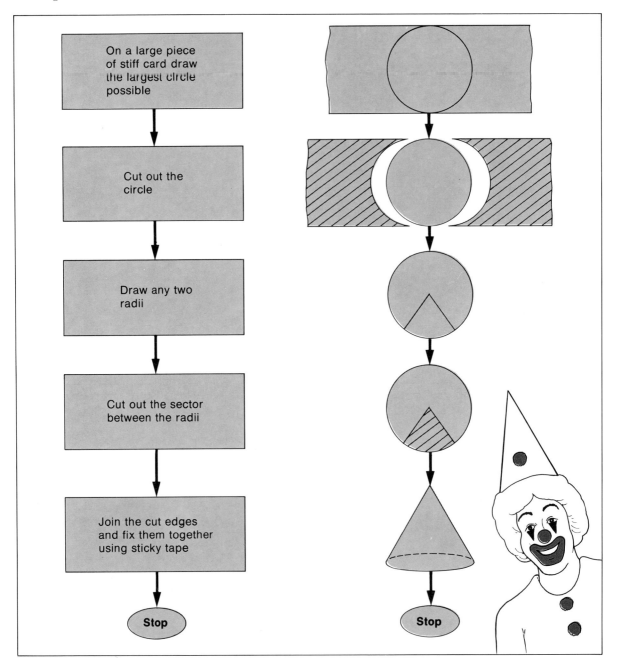

Exercise 16

Find out how to calculate the size of each interior angle of a regular polygon. Construct a flow chart showing how to do this calculation.

Scale plans

A **scale plan** is a drawing which represents real measurements by reducing them proportionally. The proportion by which they are reduced is called the **scale** e.g. A map is a scale drawing of the area it represents.

You can have scale plans of buildings, gardens, cars, aeroplanes or of anything you can construct.

Example. A scale plan to show the layout of a luxury bungalow.

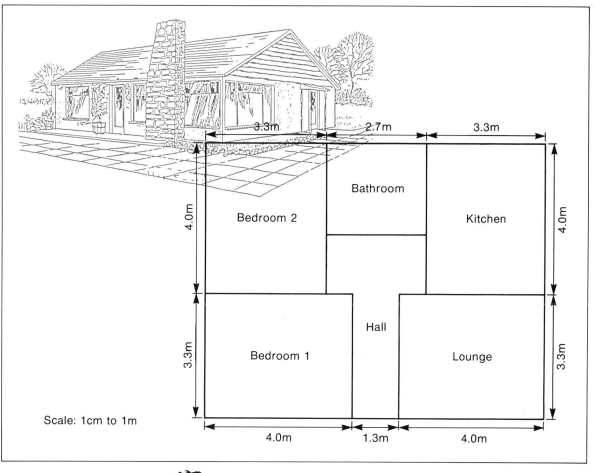

A scale plan must always show the scale

Exercise 17

Draw a scale plan of the layout of your bedroom. It should include the positions of your door, windows, bed, cupboards, etc.

Exercise 18

Design a garden. Draw a scale plan showing the layout of the lawn, flower beds, fish pond, etc.

Misrepresentation of data

Statistics may sometimes be misrepresented.

Misleading bar charts and line graphs

> The following examples show how data can be misrepresented, whether intentionally or not.

Example 1

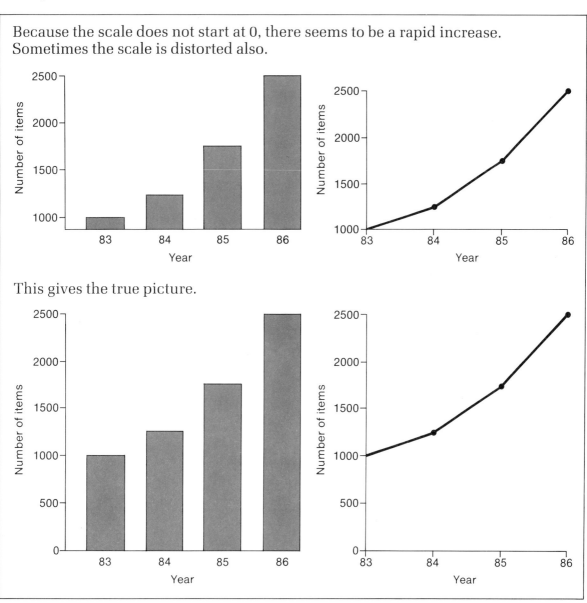

Because the scale does not start at 0, there seems to be a rapid increase. Sometimes the scale is distorted also.

This gives the true picture.

Example 2.

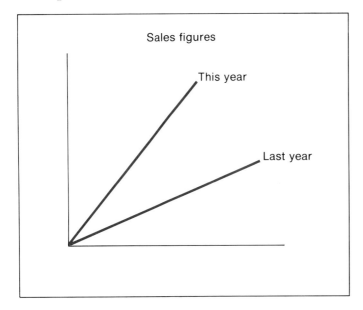

Sales figures

This year

Last year

These graphs are meaningless as there are no scales or units given.
It gives the impression that this year's sales were a lot better than last year's!

Misleading pictograms

Example.

If represents a pint of milk use to represent 2 pints.

If you double the measurements of the bottle instead, the proportion is all wrong. (In fact the new bottle has eight times the volume of the other one and should represent 8 pints.)

1 pint   2 pints   wrong

People might use this method when they want to give a misleading impression. The method is acceptable if the measurements are calculated properly so that the volumes, or areas in a two-dimensional picture, are in the correct proportion.

Exercise 19

The picture below illustrates a statement from a treasurer's report...

As you can see our takings increased greatly last month.
In fact they doubled!

Is the picture a fair representation of the statement?

Explain why you agree or disagree.

Exercise 20

For each of the graphs below say why you think the statement may not be an accurate interpretation of the graph.

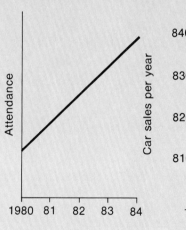

The graph shows that attendance more than doubled between 1980 and 1984

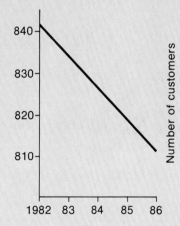

This graph proves that there has been an enormous reduction in car sales over four years

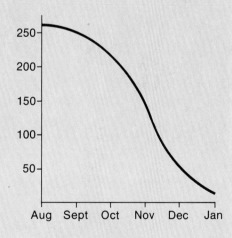

The graph shows that the standard of hairdressing is declining as less customers attend the salon

Exercise 21

Using what you have learned so far about misleading diagrams discuss these two pictures.

Exercise 22

This set of pictures represents information about the uses of water.

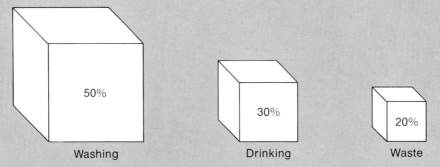

Measure the edges of the cubes.

What is, 1. the ratio of their sides,
         2. the ratio of their volumes?

Comment on how the set of pictures is misleading.

Have you thought about the most effective way of representing your information. Don't forget colour makes things look more attractive.

Have you given each table, graph and diagram a title and labelled each one clearly?

● Data can be represented in:

  – words
  – symbols
  – charts
  – diagrams
  – models.

● Charts can be:

  – bar charts
  – pie charts
  – pictograms
  – histograms.

● Diagrams can be:

  – graphs
  – number chains
  – scale drawings
  – flow charts
  – networks.

Once you have collected and represented your data the final part of your coursework task is to analyse and explain your results.

Analysis

This is making sense of your data, finding out what it means. You are trying to discover how different parts of the data link together to give an overall picture. You are asking, **'What does the data show?'**

Explanation

Explanation follows analysis. You explain the results of your analysis by finding reasons for what the data shows. You are asking, **'Why have the results turned out this way?'** Explaining the results needs a lot of thought and imagination.

Analysis and explanation in practice

The amount of analysis and explanation will depend on the task you choose. For example, the results of a survey will require a more detailed explanation than a practical task such as building a dog kennel. Sometimes presentation and analysis are very similar. When conducting an experiment or investigation you may well present and analyse your results together. Examples of analysis and explanaton are given later in this section.

ANALYSIS AND EXPLANATION

Errors

You may have made mistakes in your coursework. If you have they will affect your analysis and explanation. Be sure to check your data and note any possible errors. You don't want to be explaining something that is not true or valid.

Errors in practice

You may have some mistakes such as:

– choosing an unrepresentative or biased sample in a survey
– making an error in the timing of the traffic flow
– or simply a miscalculation somewhere in your work

– in a problem solving task you may have missed important relationships by omitting some of the variables
– in an experiment the equipment may be faulty or it may break down
– you may have come to a false conclusion by considering too few examples and not having sufficient evidence to justify a general result.

Remember, note any mistakes as they occur and say what improvements you could make.

The following examples and exercises will help you to analyse and explain your results when:

– carrying out a survey,
– conducting a simple experiment,
– investigating number patterns.

Carrying out a survey

To analyse the results of questionnaires you will need to represent the data in numerical terms.

An easy way to count answers is to follow the following method.

- Give each questionnaire a number – to make sure that you don't count someone's answers twice.
- Give each question a number – this helps you to compare different answers to the same question.
- Give each alternative answer a number – this is known as a 'code' and helps when counting.

By using this method you can transfer all the information on to a single chart which is much easier to work with. See the chart below.

The questionnaire on page 52 may have produced the following results.

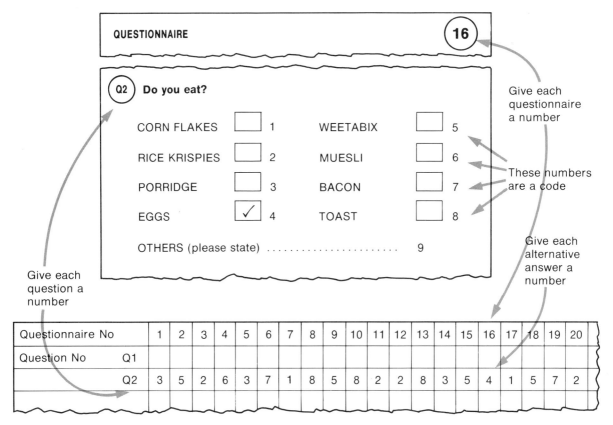

But what does **this mean**? You need to count the answers to see:

2 out of 20 eat Cornflakes
4 out of 20 eat Rice Krispies
3 out of 20 eat porridge
1 out of 20 eats an egg

4 out of 20 eat Weetabix
1 out of 20 eats muesli
2 out of 20 eat bacon
3 out of 20 eat toast

To help you **analyse** these results you may represent them with a diagram, a bar chart, pie chart or pictogram.

Example. In a bar chart

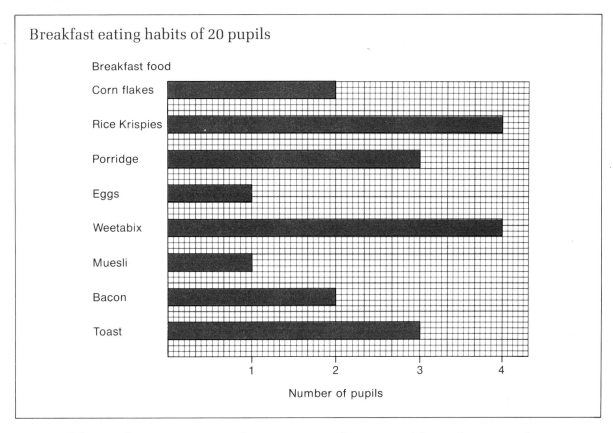

Breakfast eating habits of 20 pupils

You could now discuss your results. For example you could say that 10% of your sample eat Cornflakes, 20% eat Rice Krispies, etc. You should comment on the fact that none of your sample eat anything else for breakfast. It would be wrong, however, to conclude with this small sample, that 10% of your school eat cornflakes. It would also be wrong to make any conclusions about the eating habits of school pupils throughout the country.

To fully analyse your results you must look carefully at the responses given to other questions in the questionnaire, e.g.

   – are there any patterns in the responses
   – is one (or more) item more popular with girls than boys?

To **explain** your results you need to ask:

● Why have they turned out the way they have?
● What are the reasons for the results?

Are Weetabix and Rice Krispies the most popular because:

   – their advertising is more effective
   – they offer free gifts for younger children

Is muesli less popular because:

   – it sounds foreign
   –it tastes dry?

Are bacon and eggs less popular because:

   – they take longer to prepare
   – of the health aspect (high in cholesterol)?

If boys eat more Weetabix than girls is it because of its TV image – the Weetabix tough guys?

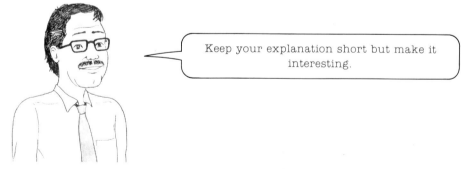

The explanation of your results can be the most interesting and rewarding aspect of your survey. Do not write too long an explanation. Remember you are writing a Mathematics not a Social Studies project. The mathematical content, presentation and analysis of the data are the most important aspects of your coursework.

ANALYSIS AND EXPLANATION

Exercise 1

Compare prescription charges with the price of drugs.

Data – collected from a secondary source.

A magazine carried out a survey of drug prices in some chemist shops. They compared for example, aspirin with a brand name drug using aspirin as a base. Three different types of drug were compared in this way.

Copy and complete the table. Give answers to the nearest 0.1p.

Name	Cost of packet	Cost of 6 tablets
Paracetamol BP Brand name	82p (100 tablets) £1.95 (72 tablets)	4.9p
Aspirin BP Brand name	62p (100 tablets) £1.49 (48 tablets)	
Paracetamol/ Codeine BP Brand name	75p (25 tablets) £2.04 (24 tablets)	

Find out the standard prescription charge. You could ask your parents, your teacher or your nearest chemist.

Representation and analysis

Draw a comparative bar chart to show how the price of 6 tablets compares for the three types of drug in the table.
Use the information from the table and chart to find the saving that could be made on a purchase of 24 tablets of paracetamol BP compared with a purchase of 24 brand name tablets containing paracetamol BP. How do each of the prices compare with the standard prescription charge?

Explanation

State briefly why you think the prices of the branded and unbranded products differ.
Can you draw any conclusion about purchasing tablets or obtaining them on prescription?

Exercise 2

BT's record big disappointment, says Which?

Formerly a State owned company British Telecom was privatised in 1984. Here are some extracts from a 'Which' report.

BRITISH Telecom's record since privatisation has been a "big disappointment" with an "alarming" one in 10 calls proving unsatisfactory because of faint or crackly lines, according to a Which? report published today. More than one in 36 calls do not get through.

The survey is based on the findings of 647 private subscribers selected at random who kept records of a total 20,369 calls during a fortnight in November.

The report commends BT for improvements made to public call boxes and welcomes competition by Mercury although it says the benefits are "probably some years off".

"It's difficult to see how, with a near monopoly on the telephone service, BT has any real incentive to improve the service it provides without greater competition or tougher regulation."

The Consumers Association calls for the telecommunications watchdog body, Oftel, to extend price controls on BT services, to establish standards of service that BT is expected to meet and to look at compensation for customers when service falls below the standards set.

In the long run, the Government should look at ways of increasing effective competition within the industry, it says.

A British Telecom spokesman said yesterday: "We know we didn't give customers a good enough service last year, but we are now well on the way to giving the best service ever."

The survey was more than six months out of date and many major service improvements forecast by Which? were already under way, he added.

Representation and analysis

Here are two of the tables produced from the collected data.

Represent this data in the form of comparative and percentage bar charts. Discuss these results. What do they show? Do you agree with the headline? What conclusions can you draw, if any, about the present service?

Delays in repairs

% of customers whose phone was repaired in time stated below

	1983	1987
Within 24 hours	41%	37%
1 to 2 days	29%	26%
3 to 6 days	18%	25%
7 to 13 days	9%	7%
More than 13 days or not repaired	3%	5%

Delays in installation

% of customers who waited this long

Time taken	1983	1987
Within a week	4%	9%
1 to 2 weeks	21%	40%
3 to 4 weeks	29%	30%
5 to 8 weeks	25%	17%
More than 8 weeks	21%	3%

Explanation

Look for reasons in the report that could explain the results. Discuss them briefly.

Questionnaires need to be looked at very carefully!

To analyse

- Present your data in a form that makes it easy to count.
- Express your results in simple mathematical terms,
- Ask:

    – how does the data fit together
    – are there any links or connections between the data
    – are there any patterns within the data?

To explain

- Ask the question, 'Why has the data produced these results?'
- Suggest reasons for:

    – the results you found
    – any unusual results
    – any mistakes you made
    – any problems you found.

Conducting an experiment

If you were doing an experiment involving the time of swing of a pendulum **your analysis** would consider the effect of component parts such as:

– the length
– the weight
– different starting positions, and so on.

Your explanation should describe the effect of changing these component parts and give clear reasons for any conclusions you may reach.
In the example which follows we have only considered the effect of changing the length of the pendulum.

In the pendulum experiment from page 45 you should have obtained a set of results similar to those shown in the table below.

Length of pendulum (cm)	0	10	20	30	40	50	60	70	80	90	100
Time for 20 swings (sec)	0	12.7	17.9	22.0	25.4	28.4	31.1	33.6	35.9	38.1	40.1

Representation and analysis

Plot the points from this table on graph paper and join them up with a smooth curve.

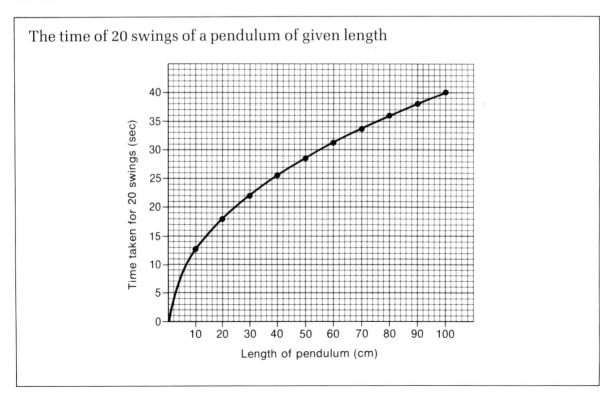

The time of 20 swings of a pendulum of given length

You should include in your **analysis**

- What the graph shows:
    - how is the time for 20 swings affected by the length of the pendulum?
- What would happen to the time if you increased the length indefinitely?
- Justifying your conclusion
    - by repeating the experiment and timing 30, 40 and 50 swings
    - by measuring the gradient of the curve for length 10, 40 and 90 cm.

In a complete analysis you would need to deal with the effect of changing other component parts such as the weight suspended, different starting positions and so on.

You should include in your **explanation**

- The conditions under which the experiment was conducted:
  - have they affected the result
  - was the whole experiment conducted under the same conditions?
- Do all the points lie on a smooth curve:
  - if not, why not?
- That the time for 20 swings increases as the length increases but gradually levels off:
  - does this levelling off mean anything?
- You should notice that as the length of the pendulum increases the gradient of the curve decreases.
- The problems, if any, you had.
- The mistakes, if any, you made:
  - did you correct them
  - were any more mistakes obvious from your analysis?
- How you would improve the experiment to obtain more accurate and useful results.

Exercise 3

Here are a set of results which a fifth year pupil obtained when she carrried out the pendulum experiment.

Length of pendulum (cm)	0	10	20	30	40	50	60	70	80	90	100
Time for 20 swings (sec)	0	13.1	17.5	23.6	25.4	28.0	31.7	33.6	35.9	38.7	40.1

Plot this set of results on the same graph paper you used in the example, on page 94. Use the same axes and compare the two sets of data. Give a brief explanation of your results.

> An experiment needs a slightly different approach!

To analyse

- Present your data in a form that illustrates it clearly.
- Ask the question 'What does the data show?'
- Express your results mathematically.
- Repeat the experiment under the same conditions as before.

To explain

- Suggest reasons for:
    - the results you found
    - any unusual results
    - any mistakes you made
    - any problems you met.

- Mention the conditions under which the experiment was conducted.

Conducting an investigation

In an investigation, analysis and explanation occur together. You are not explaining your results as you would in a survey or when conducting an experiment. In an investigation you must explain what you are doing and why you are doing it at each stage of the analysis.

> We will now consider two investigations that lead to diffent methods of analysis.

In Example 1 we look at the pattern in numbers, whereas in Example 2 the analysis also includes looking for pattern in shapes as well as in numbers.

Example 1. Investigating patterns in numbers. The **aim** of this investigation is to discover the pattern formed by adding a pair of consecutive triangle numbers.

Discovering a pattern will help you come to a general conclusion which you may be able to express as a rule or formula.

Below is the completed table which you should have obtained on page 44.

Position of Triangle No.	Triangle Numbers	Result
1st + 2nd	1 + 3	4
2nd + 3rd	3 + 6	9
3rd + 4th	6 + 10	16
4th + 5th	10 + 15	25
5th + 6th	15 + 21	36
6th + 7th	21 + 28	49
7th + 8th	28 + 36	64
8th + 9th	36 + 45	81
9th + 10th	45 + 55	100

How can we analyse these results

Let's look for a pattern.

What kind of numbers are the numbers in the results column?

This table can be rewritten in a simpler form which makes it easier for us to see if there are any patterns.

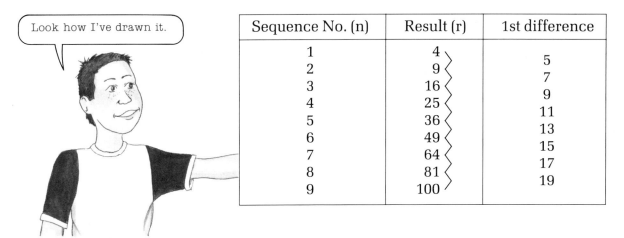

Look how I've drawn it.

Sequence No. (n)	Result (r)	1st difference
1	4	
		5
2	9	
		7
3	16	
		9
4	25	
		11
5	36	
		13
6	49	
		15
7	64	
		17
8	81	
		19
9	100	

Notice that the numbers in the 1st difference column increase by 2 each time. From this you should be able to continue the table.

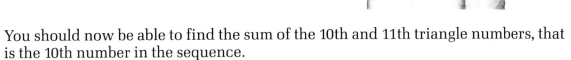

The next number in the difference column is 19 + 2, that is 21.

You should now be able to find the sum of the 10th and 11th triangle numbers, that is the 10th number in the sequence.

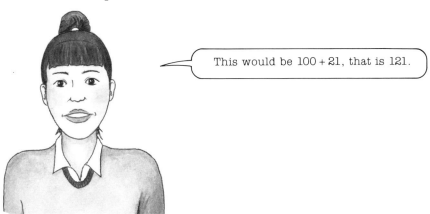

This would be 100 + 21, that is 121.

Now use the pattern to work out the sum of the 11th and 12th triangle numbers.

Could I use the same method to work out the sum of the 99th and 100th triangle numbers? This could take a long time. Is there a shorter way?

Could I work out this result **without** continuing the table?

Did you notice that the set of numbers in the results column is the set of **square numbers**? Does this help?
(The first square number is missing. Can you explain why?)

To work out the sum of the 99th and 100th triangle numbers you could look for a relationship between the sequence number (n) and the result (r). Since the result (r) is a member of the set of square numbers your first thought might have been that multiplying the sequence number by itself gives the correct result, that is, $r = n^2$

But have you jumped to a false conclusion?

I need to think about this!
Let's look more closely.

What has gone wrong?

Check

If $n = 5$
$n^2 = 25$
But if we look in the table,
when $n = 5$, $r = 36$

If we look again at the table we see that the first number in the sequence gives the result 4, which is 2^2. This may be written $(1 + 1)^2$.
The second number in the sequence gives the result 9 which is 3^2.
This may be written $(2 + 1)^2$.
The table could now be rewritten:

Sequence No. (n)	Result (r)
1	$(1 + 1)^2$
2	$(2 + 1)^2$
3	$(3 + 1)^2$
4	$(4 + 1)^2$

Let's try adding 1 to the sequence number before squaring. Do you get the correct value for r?

Look!

When $n = 5$
$n + 1 = 6$
so $(n + 1)^2 = 36$
Now $r = 36$
which is correct.

This means that if you add 1 to the sequence number and then square it, this gives the result, so $(n + 1)^2 = r$.

This is called the **formula (or expression)** to find the sum of a pair of consecutive triangle numbers.

But how can you be sure that the formula will work to find the sum of **any two** consecutive triangle numbers?

One way to be sure is to make a prediction by calculating a result using the formula and then to check it by using some other method.

For example let's use the sequence number 16, that is the sum of the 16th and 17th triangle numbers, using the formula we would get:

$$n = 16$$
$$\text{so } n + 1 = 17$$

and
$$(n + 1)^2 = 17 \times 17$$
$$= 289$$

We now need to check that this result is correct.

The 16th number in the sequence is the 9th number, (100) plus the next seven numbers in the difference column.
That is $100 + 21 + 23 + 25 + 27 + 29 + 31 + 33 = 289$

Using the pattern of differences you have confirmed the result. Hence you can say

$$(n + 1)^2 = \boxed{\ \ r\ \ }$$

Now use the formula to work out the sum of the 99th and 100th triangle numbers.

Exercise 4
Investigate the following tile pattern. (You will need some square tiles or squared paper.)

Given data

Here is a sequence of tile patterns:

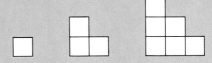

Generate more data

Build the next 3 patterns in the sequence. Count how many tiles in each pattern.

Pattern Number	Number of Tiles
1	1
2	3
3	6
4	
5	

Make a table like this and complete it.

Can you see a pattern in the numbers?

Continue the table up to pattern number 10. Do not build these patterns, but build pattern number 7 to check.

Explain how you could work out the number of tiles for larger patterns without drawing them or continuing the table.

How many tiles would you need for the 20th pattern?
Now say how many tiles you would need for the 200th pattern. Did this take a long time?

Generate further data

You could re-write the table, continuing it up to pattern number 10.

Pattern Number	Number of tiles
1	$1 \Rightarrow \dfrac{1 \times 2}{2}$
2	$3 \Rightarrow \dfrac{2 \times 3}{2}$
3	$6 \Rightarrow \dfrac{3 \times 4}{2}$

Can you discover a formula for the number of tiles used for the nth pattern number?

SECTION E

Example 2. Investigating the perimeter and area of a sequence of crosses. The aim of this investigation is to try to discover a pattern that can be expressed in a general form in order to calculate the perimeter and area of larger crosses.
On page 37 you collected data by examining the area and perimeter of a sequence of crosses.

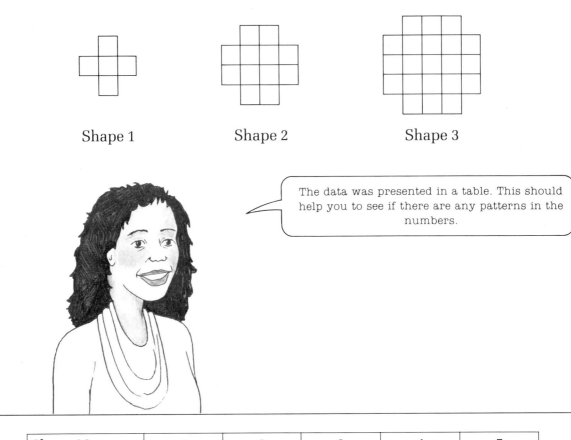

Shape 1   Shape 2   Shape 3

The data was presented in a table. This should help you to see if there are any patterns in the numbers.

Shape No	1	2	3	4	5
Perimeter	12	16	20	24	28
Area	5	12	21	32	45

(Table 1)

Investigating the perimeter

Method 1. Analysis by looking at the pattern of numbers. Can you see a pattern in the perimeter numbers?
You might have said that the perimeter numbers are all in the four times table, which is true but does not fully explain the pattern. It would be better to say that the perimeters increase by four each time starting from 12 units.

The information can be presented in a mapping diagram as shown below:

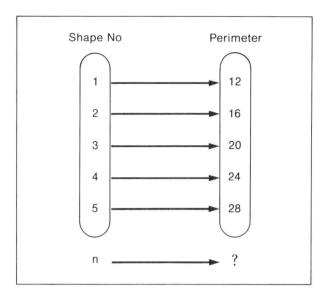

Can you generalise?

Can you express your result in a way that will enable you to calculate the perimeter of any cross shape? Can you find a relation between shape number and perimeter?

> Remembering that the perimeter numbers are all in the 4 times table you could write

Shape No.		Perimeter		
1	$\rightarrow$	3×4	$\Rightarrow$	$(1+2) \times 4$
2	$\rightarrow$	4×4	$\Rightarrow$	$(2+2) \times 4$
3	$\rightarrow$	5×4	$\Rightarrow$	$(3+2) \times 4$
4	$\rightarrow$	6×4	$\Rightarrow$	$(4+2) \times 4$
5	$\rightarrow$	7×4	$\Rightarrow$	$(5+2) \times 4$
n	$\rightarrow$	....	$\Rightarrow$	$(n+2) \times 4$

From this we can work out the perimeter for any shape number n by adding 2 to the shape number and then multiplying the answer by 4.

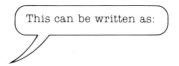

This can be written as:

$$\text{Perimeter} = 4(n + 2)$$

Now use this formula to work out the perimeter of the 100th and the 200th cross.

Method 2. Analysis by looking at the patterns in the shapes.

Looking at the diagram for shape 3 we can see that there are 4 *edges* each of length 3 units and 4 *corners* each of length 2 units.
Adding these together gives the perimeter which can be written as $(4 \times 3) + (4 \times 2)$.

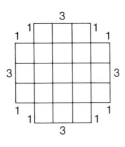

Shape 3

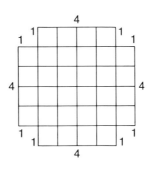

Shape 4

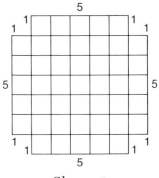

Shape 5

Shape 4 has 4 edges each of length 4 units and 4 corners each of length 2 units. This could be written $(4 \times 4) + (4 \times 2)$ units. Similarly shape 5 has a perimeter of length $(4 \times 5) + (4 \times 2)$ units.

Looking now at shape n, we can see that there are 4 edges each of length n units and 4 corners each of length 2 units, i.e. $(4 \times n) + (4 \times 2)$ units.

Shape n

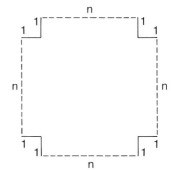

This can be written as:

Perimeter = 4n + 8

Now use the formula to calculate the perimeter of the 100th and 200th cross. Check this against your previous calculations.

From these two results we have obtained for the perimeter it follows that...
$$4(n + 2) = 4n + 8$$

Yes, I see what you mean! We could illustrate this with a rectangle.

2 units   n units

4 units   8   4n

(2+n)

$$4(n + 2) = 4n + 8$$

Investigating the area

Method 1. *Analysis by looking at the pattern of numbers*.
Look back at table 1 page 104.
Can you see a pattern in the area numbers?
You might have said that the areas increase by odd numbers each time.

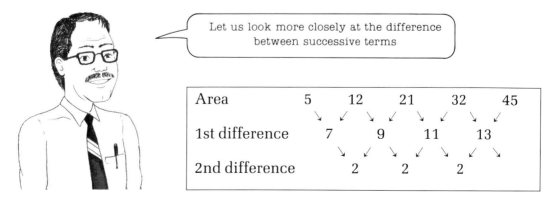

Let us look more closely at the difference between successive terms

Area	5		12		21		32		45
1st difference		7		9		11		13	
2nd difference			2		2		2		

Looking at the first difference row you will see the set of odd numbers
7, 9, 11, 13 . . .

Now looking at the second difference row we can see a constant difference of 2.
This tells us that the first difference row increases by 2 each time.

A better way of explaining the area pattern might be to say that the differences of
the area pattern or sequence, starting at 7, increase by 2 each time.

You could now calculate the next area numbers. The 6th in the sequence is
45 + 15 = 60 and the 7th is 60 + 17 = 77 and so on.

o o o

But would it be reasonable to use this method to
find the area of the 100th or 200th cross.

Can you generalise?

Can you find the area for any shape number n?

In your analysis you may have noticed when
looking for pattern that area and shape numbers
are related in the following way.

Shape	1	2	3	4	5..........
	$\downarrow \times 5$	$\downarrow \times 6$	$\downarrow \times 7$	$\downarrow \times 8$	$\downarrow \times 9$
Area	5	12	21	32	45..........

Which can be re-written like this.

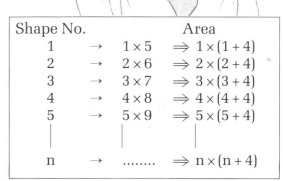

Shape No.			Area
1	$\rightarrow$	1×5	$\Rightarrow 1 \times (1 + 4)$
2	$\rightarrow$	2×6	$\Rightarrow 2 \times (2 + 4)$
3	$\rightarrow$	3×7	$\Rightarrow 3 \times (3 + 4)$
4	$\rightarrow$	4×8	$\Rightarrow 4 \times (4 + 4)$
5	$\rightarrow$	5×9	$\Rightarrow 5 \times (5 + 4)$
n	$\rightarrow$	....	$\Rightarrow n \times (n + 4)$

From this table we can work out the area for any shape number n by adding 4 to the shape number and multiplying the answer by the shape number.

This can be written as:

$$\textbf{Area} = \textbf{n(n + 4)}$$

Use this formula to work out the area of the 100th and 200th cross.

Method 2. Analysis by looking at the patterns in the shapes. The diagrams below show one of the ways of visualising how the area of each cross may be split up. Looking at shape 3 we can see that there is a 3 by 3 square in the centre with a rectangle of area 3 units attached to each side.

Adding these together gives the area which can be written as . . .

$(3 \times 3) + (4 \times 3)$ units^2.
Similarly shape 4 and shape 5
produce areas that can be written
$\qquad (4 \times 4) + (4 \times 4)$ units^2
and $\;\; (5 \times 5) + (4 \times 5)$ units^2.

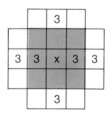

Shape 3

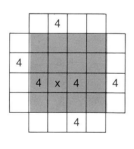

Shape 4

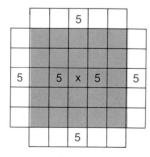

Shape 5

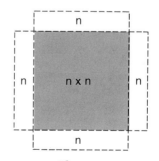

Shape n

Looking now at shape n, we can see that there is an n by n square in the centre with a rectangle of area n units attached to each side.

Adding these together gives the area as:

$$(n \times n) + (4 \times n)$$
which is the same as

$$n^2 + 4n$$

i.e. $\mathbf{A = n^2 + 4n}$

Use this formula to calculate the area of the 100th and the 200th cross. Check this against your previous calculation.

Look at the two ways I've found of obtaining the area.

$$n(n+4) \text{ and } n^2 + 4n$$

$$\mathbf{so\ n(n+4) = n^2 + 4n}$$

Exercise 5
Represent the above formula as the area of a rectangle similar to the perimeter formula on page 107.

Exercise 6
Look again at table 1 page 104

Shape no. (n)	1	2	3	4	5
Perimeter (P)	12	16	20	24	28

Plot a graph with n along the horizontal axis and P along the vertical axis. (Use a scale of 2 cm to 1 unit on the horizontal and 2 cm to 5 units on the vertical axis). Extend your graph and use it to find the perimeter of the 8th and 10th shapes. Is this another way of analysing your data?
Discuss this method briefly.

Exercise 7

Building squares.

You will need some matches or cocktail sticks. Here is a sequence of square patterns.

The pattern continues with larger arrays.

Discuss briefly how you could investigate this sequence for perimeter, area and the number of matches required to build each array. Say how you would present, analyse and explain the data.

The two investigations analysed show how we can discover a rule by looking for pattern. However there are many different types of investigations such as 'Happy Numbers' on page (73) Section D where sequences can be generated and represented by diagrams but are not necessarily connected by a general rule.

> In an investigation be sure your analysis is clear and your conclusion is valid.

- Explain what you are doing as you do it.
- Give reasons for what you do, or for any statement you make.
- Don't jump to conclusions too quickly, think very carefully about what your results show.
- Look for a general formula (or expression)
- Record failures as well as successes.
- Relate your explanation to the task you had to do, or the problem you had to solve.
- Mention other interesting facts you discover and suggest how they could be developed further.
- Remember that visual presentation through the use of models, diagrams, charts and computer graphics can greatly help with analysis and explanation.

So far we have looked at the various aspects of a coursework task. Now it is time to see how they all fit together. This section is split into 3 parts. Parts 1 and 2 are concerned with planning and carrying out the task. Part 3 deals with the final presentation.

Not everything in this section will be appropriate to every piece of work. It is designed to cover any task you may choose.

Part 1 Assignment planner

This planner will form a useful guide for planning and carrying out your assignments. It will also give you an indication of some of the things teachers will look for when marking your work.

1 Find and choose your task ▶

What shall I do?

- 'Brainstorm' ideas.
- Develop a 'resource bank' of ideas.
- Choose something:
    - that interests you
    - that you know something about
    - with easily available data
    - that can be done.

PUTTING IT ALL TOGETHER

2 Strategy ▶

How should I set about it?

- Plan your task carefully.
- What are you setting out to do?
- How will you start?
- How will you continue?
- What end do you hope to reach?

3 Choosing data ▶

What data do I need?

- Select your data carefully,
  - do not waste time collecting useless information or data which needs too much sifting through.
- Have you chosen the right data,
  - is it up to date
  - is it reliable
  - is it free from bias?

4 Collecting data ▶

How do I collect the data?

- From a Primary Source
  - an experiment
  - an investigation
  - a questionnaire
- From a Secondary Source
  - newspapers/magazines
  - official statistics
  - holiday brochures
  - text books.
- Which method will be quickest?
- Which method will give you what you want?

5 Equipment ▶

Do I need any equipment or material?

- For an experiment
  - have you all the apparatus you need?
- For a survey
  - have you enough questionnaires?
- For an investigation
  - will card, paper, scissors help?
- Is there equipment/material available which will make your task easier?
- Could you use any equipment or material to enhance the presentation of your task?
  - do not use complicated equipment/materials just because they 'look good' or seem 'impressive'.

Part 2 Carrying out the task

Do not attempt to write up your assignment task as you go along. You will not be able to see how it fits together until you have finished. Keep clear notes including diagrams of what you have done in case you forget what happened. Remember that everything that happens while you are carrying out your task is important. Writing about these things and the problems you have faced will show your teacher how your thinking has developed and how you have faced up to any difficulties you may have encountered. Look after your notes very carefully. Get a file in which to keep all your coursework material. Collect information gradually and be prepared to change your plans in the light of your findings.

1 Accuracy ▶

Have I got it right?

- Have you made sure that your calculations are correct?
- Have you thought about how accurate any measurements need to be?
- Are you certain about your information? Check it, seek advice as it may cause other parts of your assignment to go wrong.
- Have you checked for and corrected careless mistakes as you worked through your assignment?

2 As your assignment develops ▶

How does it look so far?

- Do the results of your research/investigation so far mean anything?
- Are they important to your task?
- Should you change anything at this stage because of what you have found?
- Do not be afraid to adapt, change or rearrange things if you are confident with your results.

3 Patterns ▶

Can I spot any links or connections?

- Have you looked for patterns and written about any you have discovered?
- Are the patterns you have discovered meaningful to the task?
- Remember that patterns occur in number, measurement, statistics, shape and algebra.

4 Prediction ▶

Can I see where my results are leading?

- Has your research/investigation led you to form predictions and to test them?
- Did a pattern or situation encourage or prompt you to make a prediction? Did you then check it?
- As a result of the work you have done, did you discover anything not directly concerned with your assignment which could be investigated at another time?

5 Generalisation ▶

Do my results lead to a general statement?

- Can you come to any general conclusions backed up by your results/findings?
- Can you explain these conclusions clearly in words?
- In an experiment or an investigation
  - can you present your conclusions in a mathematical form, that is, a rule or formula
  - did you test your rule
  - are you satisfied that it always works?

So much to think about . . .
but what a sense of achievement!

6 Depth of study ▶

Have I gone far enough?

- Did you achieve your aim?
- Have all aspects of the problem been fully explored?
- Have you answered the question?
- Have you done what you set out to do?
- Have you missed any important things out which you should have considered?

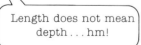

Length does not mean depth . . . hm!

When do I stop . . . what do I leave out?

Part 3   Writing up your task

Remember that your write up is the final product of your work and it is on this that you will be assessed. It is therefore important that this write up should give evidence of your planning and thinking as your assignment developed. Write your project in rough first so that your final version will be neat.

Here are some general points to keep in mind.

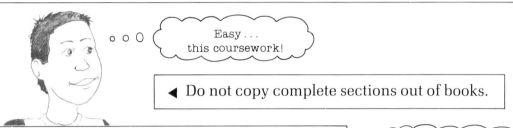

Easy... this coursework!

◀ Do not copy complete sections out of books.

Ask yourself if someone else could follow what you have written. ▶

Seems readable to me.

This looks good!

Make your coursework look as attractive as possible: ▶ include graphs, diagrams, pictures, cartoons, newspaper and magazine articles, and other visual material. Take some relevant photographs and include them. Remember to label clearly all visual material.

Where is that histogram?

◀ Place all diagrams, charts etc. correctly in the text; it makes reading and marking easier.

◀ Make sure your write-up is really relevant to what you set out to do.

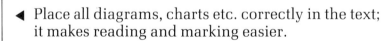

Patterns...   Numbers...
Drawings...   Formulae.

Remember that if you decide to write an essay it ▶ must have some 'mathematical' content.

Your write up should include some of the following points depending on the nature of your task.

- A title (what you propose to do).
- Why you chose the task.
- An explanation of what you did. Why you chose a particular method. How you collected your data.
- All mathematical calculations appropriate to the task with reasons for their use.
- The problems you had in carrying out the task.
- Your results illustrated by tables, charts, nets, drawings, or graphs as necessary.
- An analysis and explanation of your results.
- Any arguments used and conclusions reached.
- Any ideas for further development.
- A bibliography/sources of reference (particularly for an extended piece of work).
- Numbering the pages and adding a table of contents when you are ready to hand your coursework in.

The advantages of this approach are:

- It organises your work.
- It shows development of skills such as:
  - analysis
  - problem solving
  - decision making
  - evaluation
  - communication
  - presentation.
- It makes your coursework easier for someone else to follow.

Remember that whatever you choose for your assignment task you should present your work in a neat, imaginative and interesting way.
Good luck!

SECTION G

You have now developed the skills needed to carry out a coursework task.

Here are six sample tasks. You may wish to choose one of these as part of your GCSE coursework.

Knock-out competition	– Arrange the competitors so that you finish with just two finalists.
Space invaders	– Investigate the scales on the body of each invader!

Loop glider	– Construct the 'best' paper loop glider you can by experimenting with a basic design.

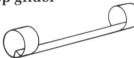

Design a computer desk	– Design and cost your own desk and compare it with 'ready made' desks.

Household chores	– How much does it cost to run a home?
Magazines	– Who likes what?, that is the question! Design a questionnaire. Visit newsagents to obtain information.

There is sufficient scope in these tasks for you to demonstrate the wide range of skills you have developed while working through this book.

Task 1 Organising an event - Knock out competition

General aim

To organise a hockey or soccer tournament amongst all the schools in your area. There are a large number of schools and you have to narrow them down to just two finalists.

Points to consider

- How will you organise the teams?
    - a straight knock-out tournament
    - dividing teams into groups.
- Time factor of whole tournament.

Data to collect

- The number of teams.
- The number of pitches available.

Data to generate

- The number of matches to be played.
    - In a knock-out tournament; how many 'byes' and why?
    - If using groups; how many groups, how many teams in each group?

For example, investigate the number of matches required for different numbers of teams in a straight knock-out tournament. Begin with a small number, say 8, and increase the number gradually. Are certain numbers of teams easier to organise? If so, why?

Representation of data

You could present your results in a series of tables showing how you worked out the order of play.
A tree diagram would be useful to show the path to the final.

What will I do with seven teams?

ROUND 1   FINAL   WINNERS

Analysis and explanation

Compare the two methods for number of games played, ease of arrangement, time to complete. Try to find a general rule or rules that would allow you to calculate the number of matches required quickly.

Task 2 An investigation - Space invaders

General aim

To investigate a sequence of numbers and try to discover a pattern in that sequence.

This is the data you are given

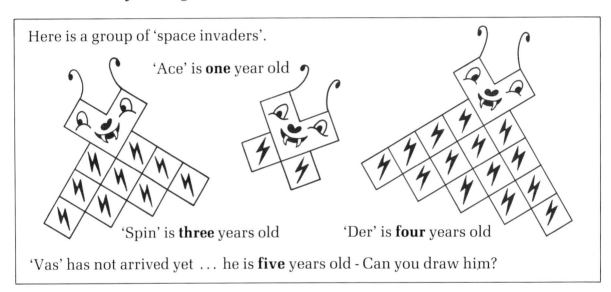

Here is a group of 'space invaders'.

'Ace' is **one** year old

'Spin' is **three** years old   'Der' is **four** years old

'Vas' has not arrived yet ... he is **five** years old - Can you draw him?

Describe how you tell the age of these space invaders.

Generate further data

Count the scales on the body of each invader. Can you see any pattern? How many scales should a **two** year old have?
Make a table to show the number of scales each invader has. Extend your table to include a **ten** year old.

Age of invader	1	2	3	4	5	6	7	8	9	10
Number of scales	2		9	14						

Investigate a method of determining the number of scales a **twenty** year old will grow.

Extension

Can you discover a rule for telling how many scales would be grown by a space invader of **any** age. (They can live for **thousands** of years!!!)

Task 3 Conducting an experiment - Loop gliders

General aim

To construct the best loop glider

> By experimenting with this basic design and altering various dimensions construct the **best** paper loop glider you can. Best means the one that flies for the longest time.

1. This design is made of 2 loops (a) and (c) together with a triangular tube (b).

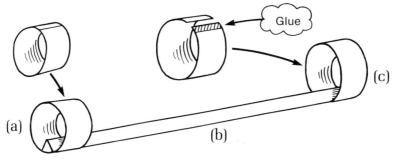

Glue

(c)

(a)

(b)

2. Each of the sections (a), (b) and (c) have been made from rectangles which are shown below.

> Go on, make it and fly it!

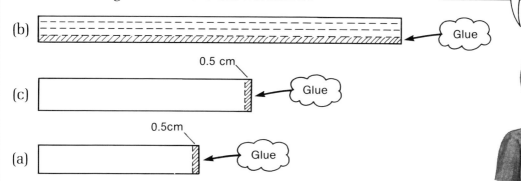

(b)

Glue

0.5 cm

(c)

Glue

0.5cm

(a)

Glue

Rectangle (b) should be made into a triangular 'tube', and rectangles (a) and (c) used to make the loops, which are then glued to the tube (b).

Collection of data

Experiment by keeping any two **lengths**, say (a), (b) constant, and altering the third length (c). Measure the time of flight accurately (make several observations and calculate the mean time). Repeat this keeping (a) and (c) constant and so on.

Representation of data

Present your results in tabular form.

Analysis and explanation

Compare the times of flight with the lengths of the various parts of the glider. Construct your 'best glider'. Explain how you think each part influences the time of flight.

Extension
What would happen if you altered the *widths* of (a), (b) or (c)?

Task 4 A practical task – Design a computer desk

General aim

To design a computer desk and to decide is it cheaper to buy or to make one?

Design your own computer station with a:
- raised stand for the monitor,
- working surface,
- open storage,
- your own special features.

Points to consider

- Type of material, e.g. teak effect, melamine finish, solid wood.
- Positioning of hardware and software.
- Stability of unit.
- Position of leads.
- Comfort and ease of use - leg room etc.
- Stationary or on wheels.

Data to collect

- Cost of materials – size of purchased lengths against wastage.
- Size of working surface and any other dimensions which you feel are important to your design.
- Purchase of materials
    - compare prices of different materials
    - compare prices from different shops.
- Prices of commercially produced units.
    - compare prices from different shops

Representation of data

Design it

- Draw a rough sketch of your design showing,
    - front elevation,
    - end elevation
    - and plan.
- Explain the main features of your design.
- Draw an accurate scale plan of your design.
- Where possible draw other suitable diagrams, tables, or charts.

Analysis and explanation

Cost it

Compare and contrast the price lists for two types of material, e.g. solid pine and melamine.

Compare it

Compare commercially designed units (possible home assembly) with your own design. Include:
- price
- strength
- quality
- suitability
- size
- attractiveness

STANDARD

DELUXE

SUPER

State what conclusions you have reached and why.

Extension

Make a suitable scale model of your design. Or, ask the Craft, Design and Technology department if they would provide the wood to make a 'real' one.

Task 5   An everyday situation - Household chores

General aim

To investigate the costs that would be involved in running a household if full labour cost had to be paid.

Collection of data

Over a period of time, say a month, keep a careful record of all work done in your household and the time taken.

Remember to include tasks such as . . .

Washing dishes

Mowing the lawn

Looking after pets

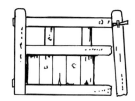
Mending the garden gate

Using local newspapers or your job centre try to find out what the rates of pay are for the different jobs you have listed.

Generate Further Data

Group together similar household tasks into broad categories for example, gardening, maintenance, and work out the average amount of time spent per week on each.

Now work out the wage bills for these using the information you obtained from the newspaper or job centre.

Representation of Data

There are many ways of representing this data ... tables, pie-charts, bar charts, composite bar charts. Choose which you think the most appropriate to show your data.

Analysis and Explanation

It's not fair. I get all the rotten jobs.

What is the total weekly wage bill for the work done in your household? Could the wage earners in your family afford to pay the staff who would be needed? Who does most of the unpaid work?
What practical difficulties arise when this type of research is undertaken?

Extension

Compare the time taken for household tasks with time taken for other things such as recreation, eating, homework, etc. How could you manage your time most effectively?

Task 6 Conducting a survey - Magazines

General aim

To discover the popularity of different magazines related to cost, age and gender of the purchasers.

Newsagents stock many different kinds of specialist magazines. Do they actually supply what people want?

Collection of data

- Go to a well stocked newsagent and choose several magazine titles.
- Visit a variety of newsagents in different localities to compare the number of your chosen magazines on their shelves.
- Note the cost of each magazine.
- Design a questionnaire, or compile a checklist of questions for the purposes of an interview.
- Choose a representative sample of pupils and parents to interview, or to answer your questionnaire.

Representation of data

How do I now present my findings?

Break the different types of magazine up into categories (weekly, monthly, quarterly) and present your results in a suitable diagram (s).

Analysis and Explanation

What is the most popular magazine? Do newsagents satisfy local needs? How does cost effect popularity? Do pupils and parents have similar tastes?

Extension

Find out which magazines are purchased for your school and how these choices are made. Ask your school librarian, subject teachers etc., for this information.